SUNDERLA

IN THE

FIFTIES

by Mel Kirtley

ACKNOWLEDGEMENTS

I wish to thank the management and staff of the *Sunderland Echo* for their assistance with the publication of this book.

Without the cooperation of the *Sunderland Echo* it would have been impossible to have recalled in such detail the events from Sunderland In The Fifties which influenced the lives of so many Wearsiders.

I am indebted to Stuart Bell, Managing Director of Northeast Press (publishers of the *Sunderland Echo*), for allowing me access to the company's archive material.

Mel Kirtley
1998

All photographs are reproduced by kind permission of the Sunderland Echo.

Typeset and layout design by Tracy Robertson and Karen Sidney.
Cover design by Stuart Bell.

Published by Wearside Books.

Copyright 1998 Wearside Books.

ISBN 0 9525380 4 0.

INTRODUCTION

The fifties represented a time of rapid change in the everyday lives of British people.

In the aftermath of war, there was an unprecedented yearning for a brighter future and the new found feelings of optimism at that time were ably demonstrated during the Festival Of Britain celebrations in 1951 and the Coronation of Queen Elizabeth II in 1953.

Slowly but surely, living standards began to rise while unemployment was at its lowest level for years. The general mood of optimism was further enhanced by the building of more houses, factories and shops than ever before.

However, against the backdrop of hope for the future, there still remained some grim reminders of war. Bomb sites were very much a part of the landscape, many foods were rationed and threats existed of further hostilities. During the early fifties, the Egyptians seized control of the Suez Canal while Hungary tried to rid itself of Russian influence. The Korean War took its toll on British troops and simmering tensions of renewed conflict between U.S.A. and Russia introduced the horrifying possibility of nuclear weaponry.

On the positive side, the seeds of the social revolution were sown and the growth of the movement was catalysed by the technological advances of the western world as Britain freed itself from the dogma of the classist society and basked in the promises of the new opportunities afforded to it by a brave new world.

The country's expanding economy was unquestionably led by the young people of the day and their rapidly growing spending power fired by tastes for fashionable clothes, records and other consumer goods. A new generation of young people who were determined to do their own thing demonstrated a new spirit of adventure and rebellion which was to change attitudes forever.

As the decade drew to a close, ordinary working class people began to develop an appetite for luxury items such as televisions, washing machines, refrigerators and even holidays abroad. It would not be too long before the car exerted its dominance on everyday life.

As Prime Minister Harold Macmillan told the nation of the time, "You've never had it so good."

The affluent society was about to arrive.

Flyleaf Caption
Fifties fashion, fifties cars and tram lines at Holmeside in 1952,
while a tram leaves Villette Road for Southwick circa *1951.*

The Sunderland Echo

Six O'clock

(77th YEAR) **and Shipping Gazette**

No. 24,397   MONDAY, January 2, 1950.   ONE PENNY

TWO-YEAR-OLD LETTER FOR JESSIE

Brings Romance to Whitburn Girl

MISS JESSIE BENJAMIN

COVERED with postmarks of Middle East and home RAF stations, a letter was thrust into the hands of 30-year-old green-eyed airwoman Jessie Benjamin, of May Grove, Whitburn, at her Air Force unit in Topcliffe early in December.

The date on the letter was two years old. It had been addressed to RAF Station Dishforth, only 25 miles away, but in the five years since she was stationed there Jessie had been at many other units both in the United Kingdom and abroad.

"Are you married yet? Why not spend a holiday here in the States.—Johnny," she read.

A cable was flashed across the Atlantic to departmental store and motor car dealer John E. Thigpen (31), an ex-G.I., of Montgomery, Alabama.

On December 21, Jessie, with the letter and a special leave pass from the RAF in her bag joined the Pan-American clipper at Heath Row and a few hours later when she stepped from the plane ex-G.I. Johnnie Thigpen was waiting with a car to take her on the last stage of her journey to Montgomery.

WELCOME

She wrote to her mother about the wonderful welcome she had been given and then she had joined the RAF in 1943 when Jessie was working as a parachute assistant in County Antrim and she met Johnnie, who was in one of the first contingents of U.S troops to come to Europe.

"Johnnie asked Jessie to marry him and when she came home after the death of her father early in 1944 she made inquiries about a passage to the States.

NEW LIFE

"And there it rested until Johnnie's two-year-old letter arrived. In the meanwhile Jessie was demobbed from the RAF in September, 1947, but she could not settle at home after seven years in the WAAF and she re-enlisted in June, 1948."

The final chapter in the story will be written shortly when Jessie returns home for her discharge from the Service to start her new life in Montgomery.

P.M. Back at No. 10: Election Pointers

THE Prime Minister, Mr C. R. Attlee, drove back from Chequers to 10 Downing Street to-day and has this afternoon attending a meeting there of a Cabinet Committee.

But no Cabinet meeting has yet been fixed and no arrangements have been made for a talk between Mr Attlee and Mr Morrison on election matters, reports the Press Association's lobby Correspondent. Nevertheless they are expected to meet to-morrow, which is the birthday of both of them.

The Prime Minister will then be 67 and Mr Morrison 62.

In authoritative quarters it is denied that there is any connexion between the general election and the return to-day of Mr Attlee to London, or the fact that five Labour M.P.s are elevated to the Peerage in the New Year's Honours List.

It has been assumed that the by-elections now caused will not be fought because of the nearness of the general election.

Meanwhile a small committee of Ministers is at work framing the King's Speech for the opening of the session of Parliament which begins on January 24.

The draft will have to be approved by the Cabinet and then sent to the King for his approval. Even when these formalities have been completed it will still be open to the Prime Minister to dissolve Parliament without a re-assembly.

He is not expected to do this and the election is still believed to be most likely either at the end of February or early in March.

Accused of Snatching Handbags

Accused of attempting to steal a handbag from a woman in Ann Lane and of stealing a bag and its contents valued at £2 1s 4d from a 73-year-old woman while she was walking along Park Road, John George Wilkinson (43), of Christopher street, was remanded in custody until Wednesday by Sunderland magistrates to-day.

In the Pann Lane case, Chief Det.-Inspector W. R. Taylor said Mrs Dorothy Davison was walking along the Lane from High Street about 5.55 p.m. on December 29 when she felt a tug at her bag. She screamed as a man ran down Pann Lane. The handle of her bag was broken and it was later found at the bottom of the Lane.

THE WRONG KIND!

BARROW-BOY Robert Davis, of Columbus (Ohio), was told by a friend that when he applied for a 1950 pedlar's licence he would need to produce two photographs.

"The kind you get at the dime store will do," he was told.

When Davis's application was sent to the City auditor it contained two photographs from the dime store —of a film star.

New Post for Mr Lawson

Mr Jack Lawson, Labour M.P. for Chester-le-Street, has been granted the Chiltern Hundreds, following his acceptance of the post of Vice-Chairman of the National Parks Commission.

Mr Lawson, who is a former Secretary of State for War, was obliged to resign his seat as an M.P., as the post is an office of profit under the Crown.

He has been M.P. for Chester-le-Street since 1919. His 1945 majority was 23,560.

There is no news of a by-election to date.

WEEK'S REMAND

William Edward Evans (27), of Orchard Street, Greenheys, Manchester, was at Manchester to-day remanded in custody for one week, charged with the murder of Thomas Wood, Gotha Street, Ardwick, on Friday.

Search Goes On

Intensive search continued at dawn to-day for the five-year-old Wolverhampton boy, Samuel James Poole, who disappeared from home on Christmas Day.

Chief Inspector Thomas Marsh, of Wolverhampton C.I.D. is again in charge of the search, which yesterday ranged over a three-mile radius from the boy's home at Goodyear Avenue, Low Hill, Wolverhampton.

Scores of uniformed and plain-clothes police with Boy Scouts, have joined in the hunt.

To-day local parks, waste land, allotments, and part of a new housing site are being combed.

PHONEVISION WILL MEAN—

PHONEVISION (movies by telephone with the aid of a television set) will quadruple film production, says Eugene F. McDonald, President of Zenith Radio Corporation, in an interview at Hollywood.

Co-Stars With Whittle in Jet Film

A SUNDERLAND man will "co-star" with Sir Frank Whittle, the prime figure in the development of the turbo-jet engine, in a Central Office of Information film showing in a Sunderland cinema on January 23.

He is Mr William Evelyn Patrick Johnson, managing director of Power Jets Research and Development, Ltd., who, as a great friend of Whittle, played an instrumental part in the development of the jet engine.

Mr Johnson, who was born in Sunderland in 1902, qualified as a patent agent before he was commissioned in the RAF in 1926. Awarded the A.F.C. for his services as an instructor at the Central Flying School, he was the first man to make a "blind" flight in April, 1931.

He left the RAF in 1933 to continue with his profession. When Power Jets, Ltd., was formed in March, 1936, he became its patent advisor.

GROUND-NUTS LINE OUT OF ACTION

Part of the branch railway to Kongwa ground-nut area, Tanganyika, was swept away by heavy rains during the week-end. The line will be out of action for several days.

The railway station at Dodoma was flooded.

Several roads in Central Tanganyika cannot be used, and famine relief supplies to districts still suffering from drought are endangered. (Reuter).

COLOUR T.V.

COLOUR T.V.—Colour television has been broadcast at Washington to the homes of four members of the Federal Communications Commission which has asked for a month of test broadcasts.

Wearsiders Sing and Dance

WELL past one o'clock yesterday morning Wearsiders sang and danced in the main streets of Sunderland to welcome in the New Year. Midnight dancers from Sunderland dance halls streamed into the streets soon after 12 o'clock to join the hundreds who were waiting to hear the Town Hall clock strike 12 o'clock.

The weather was kind. Mild air kept people out-doors into the early hours of Sunday morning. The custom of first-footing was enthusiastically followed by thousands, and many lights in Wearside homes were kept burning until dawn.

Parties at home flourished for hours after public-houses and dance halls closed.

TOWN MAN'S ACHIEVEMENTS

BETTER ATTENDED

Watch-night services in Sunderland churches were generally better attended than for some years. In Bishopwearmouth Church, for instance, about 800 people attended the service which ended about a quarter past twelve.

An encouraging sign was the large proportion of younger people who went to the services. The Rev. H. M. Connop Price was particularly pleased with the number of young men and women who joined his service.

CONDEMNS ANTI-RED "POLICE STATE"

Mr J. Edgar Hoover, Chief of the Federal Bureau of Investigation — the "G-Men" who provide the American Political Security Service— to-day declares that "police state methods" to combat Communism would put the future of democracy itself in jeopardy.

"Police state methods can only encourage the growth of the very evil we abhor," he writes in a George Washington University publication.

"The American people are determined that Communism shall be rejected. However, as in years past, we again hear cries, 'Cut the red tape of formality,' 'forget about freedom of speech when talking about Communists.' 'let's cast them out.'

"These critics urge the formation of a national police, a police system which, they assert, would handle the Communist menace with dispatch and finality.'

"Such methods would "mean the tearing of law enforcement from its democratic matrix and the creation of a 'state within a state,' a law enforcement system unresponsive to the will of the majority and obeying only the dictates of the governing few." (Reuter.)

WEARSIDERS GREETED THE NEW DECADE BY SINGING AND DANCING IN THE STREETS.

In 1950 ...

Come Dancing was first transmitted on BBC Television.

Diners Club cards were launched.

USA beat England in football's World Cup competition.

Production of television sets soared by 250%.

The first kidney transplant operation was performed.

The Korean War began.

Petrol rationing ceased.

Sainsbury's opened their first self service store.

Watch With Mother was first shown on BBC Television.

Princess Anne was born.

USA proceeded with H Bomb research.

George Bernard Shaw died.

Snooker was televised for the first time.

Labour were re-elected in the closest General Election result in over 100 years.

Soap rationing finally ended on 9th September.

The population of the UK was 44.5 million.

350,000 British homes owned a television.

Left
During the fifties, there was a chain of Bamborough grocery shops in Sunderland.

Right
Competitive pricing without gimmicks at Liverpool House.

In Sunderland in 1950...

The appeal of football as a spectator sport was at its peak during the early fifties and no more so than at Roker Park where Sunderland attracted a crowd of 55,097 for an F.A. Cup tie with Huddersfield Town on the first Saturday of the new decade. The 'invasion' of Roker Park had started at 8.30am when two women accompanied by their husbands arrived at the ground and were followed by a Darlington baker who had rushed to Sunderland for the third round F.A. Cup tie as soon as he had finished a night shift at 6.30am. By noon, over five hundred people were waiting for the kick off while thousands of fans streamed over Wearmouth Bridge wearing rosettes, scarves and berets. Sunderland won the game 6-0 with two goals each by Davis, Broadis and Shackleton.

On 9th January 1950, Sunderland Corporation introduced an experimental scheme in an effort to eliminate traffic congestion in Fawcett Street. For the first time since tram lines were laid, passengers were not permitted to board southbound tramcars in Fawcett Street. The Corporation boarded up queue barriers while inspectors posted at the barriers were greeted with amazement and hostility when they advised prospective travellers that they would have to queue at alternative stops.

Above
This photograph was taken at
St. Thomas Street during 1950 when
Palmers was a major trading name in
Sunderland.

Right
Southwick tram terminus on a wet day in
November 1950.

A seventy two year old woman in Drury Lane, Sunderland was fined £5 in a Magistrates Court for keeping her home as a betting house. Although she said in court that she had never backed a horse in her life, a plain clothes policeman told the bench that during a half hour period he had seen seven men, five women and eight children visit her house. On entering the house, he had found the accused counting money and found betting slips and two bundles of ready money football coupons.

"The Dancing Years Are Over" claimed Sunderland Corporation's entertainments manager as he reported falling attendances at the town's Seaburn Hall. He commented that the urge to waltz dreamily or to perform in a conga line had lessened considerably since the dance crazy days immediately after the war when not to dance was high on the list of social crimes. He identified a reduction in purchasing power as being one of the reasons for the decline and highlighted the fact that licencees of public houses and hotels had reported their worst Christmas/New Year takings since 1939. He concluded by saying that spending power of 1949/1950 did not compare with the 'easy money days' of 1946-1948.

Above
This classic Sunderland Echo *photograph shows four dockers on their way to work in 1950.*

It was reported that coal and coke shipments from Sunderland in 1949 were the highest since 1939 with a total of 2,945,219 tons being shipped. The figure showed an increase of 154,526 tons on the previous year. Imports on the River Wear totalled 417,288 tons and were the highest since 1937 and included 119,101 tons of petroleum which at that time was a record for the Wear. Other significant imports included grain (19,232 tons), cement (22,301 tons) and chrome ore (20,930 tons); this latter product representing a rapidly developing new trade for the town.

The British people are not getting their fair share of the world's food production, alleged councillor Stephen Hudson Conservative candidate for Sunderland North. He said that while the world's meat production was only 4% below its pre-war level, average consumption of meat in Britain was down by 30% compared with 1939 levels. Meanwhile, Mr. Richard Ewart Socialist candidate for Sunderland North admitted that the quality of food was 'not as high as the privileged classes enjoyed in 1938' but he stressed that bulk buying imports had as least enabled everyone to have their fair share.

Polling in the General Election got off to a slow start in Sunderland on a wet February morning. However, as the day progressed housewives made the voting booths their first stop on the way to the shops and by late morning indications were that the turn-out would be a record one. Final figures showed that the poll was one of the highest in the town's history with 84.3% of the electorate in Sunderland North (54,416 people) and 83.2% in Sunderland South (65,833 people) going to the polls. The *Sunderland Echo* made arrangements for the results to be shown on a screen at the Havelock Cinema and the public were admitted free of charge at 10.45pm. A special edition of the *Sunderland Echo* was published at midnight to give the election results which were as follows:-

Sunderland South Division:
R. Ewart (Socialist) 27,192;　H. Wilkinson (Conservative) 22,012;　C.J. Kitchell (Liberal) 5,604.

Sunderland North Division:
F.T. Willey (Socialist) 24,810;　S. Hudson (Conservative) 17,469;　J. Hurst (Liberal) 3,614.

Sunderland's post-war housing programme was one of the most ambitious in the country. By March 1950, Sunderland Corporation had completed the construction of 3,533 post-war houses. There were 1,176 men employed on housing estates at Thorney Close, Pennywell and Hill View. It was announced in May that the town's seventh post-war corporation housing estate would be built at Castletown on a 224 acre site owned by the National Coal Board. It was estimated that the site would accommodate 1,800 houses. With Springwell estate completed and proposals to build housing at Hylton, Red House and Farringdon Hall, it was predicted that Sunderland's post-war housing total would reach 9,389 by 1952.

Thirteen faithful employees of Sunderland Corporation went to work as usual on 14th Match 1950 not knowing that as from April their services would be no longer required. The growth of mechanisation resulted in redundancy notices being served on thirteen Clydesdale horses belonging to the cleansing department. The horses together with their carts and equipment were auctioned following the arrival of a modern fleet of cleansing vehicles. The last horse to plod along Sunderland's street was George, the eldest of the faithful thirteen and remnant of a workforce of sixty two horses from 1938.

Alarm bells were set ringing when a rapid accumulation of sand at the south end of Roker beach meant that only six of the twenty two steps leading from the promenade were visible. Sunderland Corporation's Seaside Development Committee sought urgent talks with the River Wear Commissioners to investigate the problem. The reason given for the potentially serious problem was that the piers were interfering with the natural work of the tides. The balance of the tides were being upset insomuch that those tides which were sweeping many tons of sand high up on to the beach had no corresponding force to take away the accumulation.

Sunderland Corporation's Food Control Committee asked the Ministry Of Food to investigate the possibilities of fixing a definite meat standard for pies. A Sunderland councillor commented that the quantity of meat in some pies was of starvation levels and it was absurd that a manufacturer with a certain allocation of meat should be allowed to make five times as many pies as the quantities of meat dictated. Cases had been reported of some pies having as little as 7% of meat whilst Sunderland Corporation Health Committee considered that pies should contain a minimum meat content of 25%. Sunderland's barrow boys were given a stern 'clean up or else' ultimatum by the council. It was reported that the traders were leaving their bomb site pitches in a filthy state at the end of the day and the corporation's cleansing workers were having to clean up after them. The town's General Purpose Committee set about investigating whether the sites could be acquired by the corporation under Ministry Of Health legislation which gave local authorities the power to take over sites when there was little prospect of building operations for some years. The barrow boys were dealt a further blow with the news that the town's Health Committee asked the Ministry Of Health to allow the implementation of sanctions for tighter regulations governing the open air sale of food. The committee requested the inclusion of additional by-laws to those in force regarding the clean handling of food. Included in the proposals was that any land used for the sale of food should be paved with asphalt or concrete and should be effectively drained. It was also proposed that all stalls should be equipped with supplies of hot and cold water.

Sunderland town council approved a scheme to replace trams with buses on the Villette Road route.

It was announced in April that the River Wear's shipping output in 1949 was 36 vessels with a combined tonnage of 200,626 tons. This placed the Wear in third place of the largest shipbuilding centres in Britain.

Four men were each fined £1 for traffic obstruction by Sunderland Magistrates Court. Defending solicitor for one of the men said, "Towns such as Sunderland were built before the development of motor cars were ever thought of and were built for the requirements of one hundred years ago. People were faced with a terrible dilemma." His client, a local businessman, had parked his car opposite the north end of Sunderland's central railway station and a traffic jam had resulted.

Over 40% of Sunderland's 180,000 ration books remained unclaimed with less than one week before the date from which they could be used to purchase foodstuffs. It was announced that any unclaimed books would soon be available for collection from the food office in John Street.

Above

This photograph was taken from Springwell Road looking up Holborn Road circa 1950. Today, Grindon fire station stands on the site occupied by many of the prefabs.

The Ministry Of Town & Country Planning announced that the 106 year old Penshaw Monument had been included in a list of sixteen buildings classed as being of special architectural or historic interest under the Town & Country Planning Act 1947. Under the provisions of the act, listed buildings could not be demolished or altered without prior local planning permission.

Sunderland AFC's receipts from home Football League games during 1949-1950 season reached the record figure of £93,568. Gross total income for all games, including cup games and friendlies, was £128,079, which was also a record.

Sunderland Corporation coined the phrase 'Where Litter Lies - Beauty Dies' on its new litter bins at Seaburn.

When three smart girls went shopping for nylons in Sunderland, an open air trader found himself in court accused of over charging. The first girl, a telephonist from Sunderland Police Station paid 16s 11d for a pair of fully fashioned non-utility nylons from the Union Street trader and then reported the matter to the two other girls; a policewoman and a price regulation inspector. The trader was accused of over charging on the grounds that the maximum price for such nylons was fixed at 12s 11d. The trader's defence commented that his client had purchased the nylons from the type of people who The Board Of Trade can never seem to get to court. He continued to say that his client was "a victim of the inexorable search for these flimsy things which decorate the nether limbs of our women, no doubt for the delight of mortal man." The trader was fined £25 with costs.

When the 23,000 ton motor tanker *Hoegh Arrow* was launched from the shipyard of Sir James Laing in July, thousands of people turned out to see the largest ship ever built on the River Wear. As shipyard workers raised their caps and cheered, several Norwegian and Wearside school children stood on a specially constructed platform to witness the launch.

Coal shipments from the Wear for the first six months of the year were 110,592 tons up on the corresponding period of the previous year. Of the 1,526,848 tons of coal shipped, 423,745 tons were exported. Although the figure showed a healthy year on year increase, it compared unfavourably with immediate pre war figures and was 659,911 tons down on the first six months of 1938.

With one council house built for every forty two Wearsiders, Sunderland climbed into fifth position in the league table of county boroughs in England and Wales for house building per head of population.

Right
The launch of the Hoegh Arrow
in November 1950.

Within the space of one hour, three ships were launched from the River Wear on 12th September and all were for UK owners. The largest was the 8,800 ton cargo vessel *King City* built by William Doxford while a 4,600 ton steam collier was launched from the yard of William Pickersgill on the opposite side of the river. The third launch was a 3,570 ton steamer built by S.P. Austin & Son.

On a straight party vote of 41 to 14, Sunderland Town Council rejected a plea by Progressives that council house tenants should be allowed to buy their own homes.

In September, Sunderland Corporation Building Licences Committee voted to continue the ban on private house building for the third successive year. As a result of nobody in the town being allowed to build their own house, there was an inevitable increase in the number of building plans on file in readiness for the lifting of the ban. Although builders forecast an avalanche of construction orders once the ban was lifted, the heavy work load would be largely offset by a marked decrease in council house building.

Above
Sunderland's art gallery in 1950.

In December, owners of the 850 seat Villiers Electric Theatre were fined £25 for failing to show their full quota of British films. It was the first prosecution of its kind in the country. In the period under review (October 1948 - September 1949) the Villiers showed 14.07% of British films instead of the 45% minimum required by the Cinematograph & Films Act of 1948. Defending solicitor for the theatre explained that while British studios did not produce Wild West films, that was the sort of material which the Villiers' predominantly young audience wanted to see.

Ten thousand Sunderland shipyard workers benefited from a pay rise which gave them a new national uniform rate of £6 per week for skilled workers and £5 per week for the unskilled. The rates applied for the national working week of 44 hours.

Towards the end of 1950, demolition began on the Monsanto Chemical Works which first began production in Sunderland in 1930. At its peak, the company employed one hundred men and manufactured up to 20,000 tons of crude tar per year. The crude tar was converted into such derivatives as tolvol (the base product of TNT), motor spirit, anthracine, creosote and pitch. Prior to closure, the chemical works set up a record for the number of fires in the town. A Monsanto spokesman commented at the time, "We had about twenty fires here in the past few months. On such a site as this, fires are all part of the working day."

The Sunderland Echo
Six o'clock

and Shipping Gazette

(78th YEAR)

No. 24,447   FRIDAY, January 12, 1951.   ONE PENNY

HOUSE COAL CUT

Fuel Ministry Says: " 8 cwt. To Cover Months of January & February"

6 CWT. IN THE SOUTH

WEARSIDERS are to get less coal. The present winter allocation is 5 cwt. (max.) per month. To-day the Fuel Ministery said domestic coal deliveries will be restricted between January 1 and February 28 to 8 cwt.—a cut of 2 cwt.

In the Eastern, London, South-Eastern, Southern and South - Western regions coal merchants, through their organizations, have been asked to restrict the quantity to 6 cwt. to domestic premises.

This step, says the Fuel Ministry, has been taken to conserve stocks and to ensure the widest and most equitable distribution of the coal available during the coming critical weeks.

The announcement says this restriction will not affect deliveries under licences already granted, which will be met so far as supplies permit.

Up to now the allocation has been 5 cwt. per year, with 5-cwt. maximum during the winter months and 4cwt. in the summer.

Sunderland coal merchants,

Talks About 'Z' Men

THE question of calling up some of Britain's 000,000 Class Z reservists for training is being considered by a Government committee, writes a Diplomatic Correspondent.

This committee, working continuously, has completed the [blue] print for a new and accelerated defence programme under which Britain will spend more than the £3,600 million allocated for armaments last summer.

A complete revision of the whole defence programme has been made, covering production, industrial labour, finance and service manpower.

ORDERS PLACED

The new plans will come before the Defence Committee of the Cabinet shortly.

Already more than half-a-million men are engaged in this country on arms production and Government orders have been placed for tanks, aircraft and weapons of all kinds to the extent of £450 million.

Mr Attlee discussed this expansion of Britain's rearmament with President Truman in Washington and Mr Bevin, the Foreign Secretary, in Brussels this month, and gave the Atlantic Treaty Powers an undertaking that Britain would do still greater efforts for defence of the West.

FOOD MINISTER Mr Webb hinted to-day that there may be a reimposition of control if rabbit prices continue to remain high.

A " FIREBALL " HITS SHOPS

A FIREBALL meteorite shattered suburban shops when Melbourne's heat-wave broke to-day. The temperature quickly dropped 25 degrees from 104.

many of whom have already delivered customer's coal for January—and even February—are at a loss to understand how the Ministry expect them to work such a scheme.

" Two weeks of January have almost gone and in that time we have delivered large quantities of coal," said one. "Some customers get a year's supply at once and many of them get it in two-month allocations. The announcement is going to result in grave complications to our books.

" It seems very unfair that it should be made almost in the middle of the month," he added.

GROCER (80) BATTERED

Mr Frederick Gosling, nearly 80, owner of a busy grocer's shop between Chertsey and Addlestone (Surrey), was found dead to-day tied by ropes to his bed and with his head badly battered.

He had lived alone for some years. He was found by a woman who arrived to do some cleaning.

south—Flooded Roads: Scotland – Snowdrifts

ROAD reports received by the A.A. show that many roads in the Southern half of England are still flooded, but most main roads are clear.

There are still 18 inches of water at Runnymede on the Staines-Windsor Road.

In Scotland snow and ice have affected many highways in the south and east, and drifts have formed in some places.

Although the position round Oxford is easier, in some areas there are floods almost as far as the eye can see.

Some roads are flooded in the Thames Valley and there is mild flooding on minor roads in the Isle of Ely.

"NEW DEAL" CONFERENCE

A special conference of the NCB will be held at York on Tuesday or Thursday to consider the "new deal" which has been agreed between the National Coal Board and the executives. Delegates from every coalfield in Britain will be asked to implement the agreement.

Increases in pay for nearly 700,000 day wage workers in the industry, including miners at the coal-face, winding engine-men and craftsmen are estimated to cost £6 million a year.

(See Page Four)

FAT IN FIRE

Crews of three fire appliances, answering a call at Nidge to-day, found that there was in a kitchen a suet pudding had caught fire during the temporary absence of the house-

Three Women in a Bed

Three ex-Servicemen and their families last night seized the old Cutler Boulter Dispensary in Gloucester Green, Oxford — a large barn-like place which is in course of being turned by the W.V.S. into a club for American soldiers.

Because of the work going on there was only one room available and while the three women slept in one bed the three husbands and a three-and-a-half-year-old child slept on the floor.

The families have all had their names down on the Council's housing list for years.

The W.V.S. have not been able to find accommodation for the three families, and it is understood they have no intention of removing the squatters.

THE LONDON RAIL STRIKE SPREADS

drivers and cartage men at London's Nine Elms, Camden Town railway depots stopped work in sympathy with the unofficial strikers at St. Pancras.

Camden Town a strike claimed that between 400, 500 men were out, but

a Midland Region official put the figure at 290.

After a meeting at Nine Elms, Mr Bill Sayers, Branch Secretary of the National Union of Railwaymen, said that 169 of the depot's drivers and a number of vanmen, who went on strike earlier in the day, had decided to remain out.

He said that 1,000 other

workers at the depot, one of the biggest in Britain, had decided that they, too, would strike if the dispute should spread to other London depots.

The St. Pancras strikers claim that they are likely to become redundant because of the introduction of a new system of goods transport at London and Glasgow.

Chinese Planes Raid Front

EDWARD G. ROBINSON, the film "tough guy" has been assured by the United States House of Representatives Committee on Un-American Activities that it has no evidence he was ever a Communist.

ONE or more Communist bombers, disguised with American markings, to-day made at least four raids on towns along the Western front.

One was definitely identified as an American-built plane of a type of which a number were turned over by the United States to Chinese Nationalists after World War II.

Chinese and North Korean forces to-day continued to mass in two main areas in preparation for fresh assaults on U.N. defence lines—in the Osan area in the west and north and east of the rail centre of Wonju in the centre.

The United States Second Division is reported holding firm against sporadic small arms fire attacks near Wonju.

On the eastern flank, the Communists are slipping down a 10-mile-wide corridor in the direction of Taegu.

A Communist column to-day thrust wide and deep around the U.S. Second Division's east flank in a move which threatened the Americans' fighting stand round Wonju.

THE KING

The King returned to-day from Sandringham to Buckingham Palace by road. He is expected to receive Mr Attlee and Mr Liaquat Ali Khan, Pakistan Prime Minister, before returning by road to Sandringham to-morrow afternoon.

BABIES THROWN IN RIVER

BRITISH troops near the Korean front line spotted several small bodies washed up on the banks of a river.

They pondered . . . . then realized what was happening.

Hungry, foot-weary Korean women were throwing their babies and children into the river from a bridge rather than expose them to the biting cold as they trudged south, away from the Communists.

Many of the refugees congesting the roads were scantily clad, carried babies on their backs, and clutched treasured possessions. Many, too, had no food.

Some mothers, realizing their tragic plight, halted on their southward trek and stood on the bridge. Tearfully the baby was thrown into the icy river to put an end to its hardship.

Smallpox: 6th Death

DEATHS in the smallpox outbreak at Brighton now number six and the total number of cases is 24.

The sixth death, which occured yesterday, was that of Miss Pamela Morbey, a nurse from the Bevendene Hospital, Brighton.

Two cases were admitted to Foredown Isolation Hospital, Portslade, last night. They were another nurse from the hospital and a child.

"Cosy Corner" Pole Jailed

Zbigniew Kalinowski, 22-year-old Polish metalworker, of no fixed address, who at Bucks Assizes in October was acquitted of being concerned in the "Cosy Corner" murder, was at the same Court to-day sentenced to 21 months' imprisonment for breaking and entering the Cosy Corner Stores at Hazlemere and stealing £21 10s, the property of Mr William Thomas Dearlove, the murdered man. He pleaded guilty.

Mr C. J. Campion (prosecuting) said when he was being tried on the graver charge Kalinowski made certain admissions, as a result of which the present charge was brought.

A U.S. Navy patrol bomber carrying a crew of 14 crashed in the Northern Ryukyus Islands yesterday. Unofficial reports say eight were rescued, one killed, and five are missing.

POST WAR AUSTERITY REFLECTED BY RESTRICTIONS
ON DOMESTIC COAL DELIVERIES.

In 1951 ...

The Archers was first broadcast on BBC Radio on 1st January.

British diplomats Burgess and Maclean defected to Russia.

The first Miss World contest was staged.

Toni bells rang for the first time on British ice cream vans.

Ivor Novello died.

77 year old Winston Churchill was re-elected as Prime Minister.

The Goon Show started on radio.

The 33^{1}/3 rpm long playing record was launched.

An Austin A40 car cost £685.

Oxford sank in the boat race.

The average weekly earnings in Britain were £8 6s.

The Festival Of Britain celebrations were held.

GCE examinations were firsted introduced.

Stilleto heeled shoes became fashionable.

1.5 million homes in Britain owned a telephone.

Left
Remember the
Co-op in Green
Street?

Above
Words of wisdom from the doctor!

In Sunderland in 1951...

With 285 deaths in Sunderland between March 1950 and January 1951, the town's funeral directors reported one of their busiest periods in twenty years. One funeral director said that he was so busy that he could not spare time for proper meals and was eating sandwiches in his car as well as taking his work home on a night! He commented, "On average we have four or five burial orders per week but we have had eleven this week and already have seven planned for next week." The majority of deaths were reported as resulting from pneumonia following a prolonged spell of cold weather.

Above
Seaburn Hall was a popular teenage rendevous throughout the fifties.

The gloomy news which greeted Sunderland housewives in January included increases in laundry prices, rising costs of rabbits with the prediction that they could soon become luxuries, shortages of tea stocks in most grocer shops and a sharp increase in the price of gloves. To add to the gloom, dustbins had become scarce and the news was that the silver galvanised variety would soon disappear to be replaced by the black wartime type.

Ambitious plans were announced to propel Sunderland and the twin resorts of Roker and Seaburn into the 'Big Four' revenue earning local authorities in Britain. With a six figure income the target, plans included the construction of a seafront cafeteria at a cost of £3,500, a full scale military tattoo and an extended season of illuminations which was planned to run from 8th September until 20th October with firework displays four night per week. It was reported that a record income of £78,954 had been set in 1949 and although this fell slightly in 1950 due to bad weather, the corporation was confident of a new record being set in 1951 - if the sun shone!

In February 1951 demolition began on the 107 year old Church Of St. Andrew in Deptford. The church had earlier closed in 1948 under a reorganisation scheme following the movement of parishioners from Deptford to other parts of the town.

Right
St. Andrews Church in Deptford during demolition in February 1951.

The Corporation Transport Committee accepted a tender from a Leeds based company for the construction of twelve double deck buses and in doing so they annoyed a group of so called Progressives on the town council who claimed that there was a Sunderland firm of coachbuilders capable of undertaking the work. It was disclosed that the tender of the local company was only £12 per bus higher than its Yorkshire rivals and critics claimed that for the benefit of this small saving it had been wrong to discard work opportunities for the town. The chairman of the the Transport Committee made the point that the local company, Associated Coachbuilders, did have some experience of building single deck buses but none at all of building double deckers. He did promise to give them a trial at a future date to ascertain the quality of their work.

Southwick Road bridge was closed from March 1951 whilst the structure was strengthened and the road widened. Tram services were temporarily replaced by buses until the work was completed.

Thorney Close primary schools were opened for the first intake of pupils on 2nd April 1951. Places were available for 360 infants and 480 juniors.

British Railways Executive told Sunderland Corporation's General Purpose Committee that the long overdue work in connection with the re-construction of the town's central railway station - at that time regarded as Sunderland's most famous eyesore - was due to start before the end of the year.

Left
Herring drifters at South Dock, Sunderland in October 1951.

The launch took place of the 290 ft. after-end of the the first tanker in the world to be built in two parts. The half ship was launched from the Strand slipway yard of John Crown & Sons. The River Wear's smallest shipyard did not have a berth capable of accommodating so large a ship and indeed the two berths at the yard had to be joined to accommodate even the half ship. Once the Crown yard had completed the 275 ft. fore part, both halves were joined at a South Shields yard.

Left
The shipyard of
Joseph L. Thompson
& Sons at night in
October 1951.

Large scale extensions to the Pallion shipyard of William Doxford & Sons involved the demolition of two hundred houses in the Watson Street area. Sunderland Corporation announced plans to build one hundred houses in each of 1951 and 1952 to dovetail with the demolition which in turn would facilitate the shipyard's extension scheme. The extension took place at the company's engine works and was needed to cope with an increased demand for the world famous Doxford engines.

The first steps were taken to restore Hendon beach to its former glory with the long stretches of golden sand which had been familiar to the older generation of Wearsiders. Work involved the removal of wartime dumping of debris and scrap metal while rocks and shingle were also removed. It was hoped that Hendon beach would become a minor resort of the town.

As early as April 1951, a draft development plan prepared by the borough engineer revealed that Sunderland's town centre of the future would be encircled by a new inner ring road with a civic centre at West Park and principal shopping facilities grouped together. The six main proposals of the development plan involved (1) Re-siting of the central railway station, (2) construction of a new bus station immediately adjacent to the railway station, (3) grouping together of the principal shopping facilities, (4) construction of a new civic centre on an eight acre site bordered by West Park and St. George's Square, (5) three additional car parks to be built in close proximity to the new central inner ring road and (6) allocation of land for light and service industries immediately adjacent to the town centre. The corporation's Highways Committee subsequently approved the £37$^{1}/_{2}$ million fifteen year plan with the exception of housing the bus station next to the railway station.

Civilian occupiers of thirteen huts at Lizard Lane Camp, Whitburn received notice to quit the properties from Boldon UDC following instructions from the War Department who wished to take over the former military camp for training purposes.

Sunderland Industries Exhibition opened at Seaburn Recreation Ground on 11th July 1951. In opening the exhibition, Mayor Alderman W. Harvey said he hoped that the town would be as proud of 1951 in one hundred years time as it is of 1851 today. The Mayor said that Sunderland had sent ships and goods to the four corners of the world and in doing so it had achieved a position during the last one hundred years of which its people can be justly proud. "This exhibition proves that in this festival year our workmanship and industry can give us a great deal of civic pride," he said. The exhibition was part of the Festival Of Britain and had been conceived both as a selling agency for Sunderland products and as a show for townspeople to illustrate the products manufactured by a first class industrial town.

Hylton Parish Council of Castletown and Ford and the Parish Council of South Hylton staged a protest meeting in response to what was regarded as an inadequate response from Durham County Council concerning proposals to build a bridge across the River Wear at South Hylton. Durham County Council rejected the proposals which, if given the go ahead, would have removed the need for miners to travel six miles to work when they could see their pit just 1/2 mile across the river.

The potato famine of 1951 meant that a Sunderland crisp factory began laying off some of its fourteen strong workforce. Wholesalers introduced a rationing system and, in turn, the crisp factory cut supplies to both retailers and wholesalers alike. However, it was reported that some dealers had set up a black market by purchasing potatoes at prices in excess of the control price. In some cases the potato racketeers found no buyers and in such circumstances they took to outdoor potato selling on their own behalf.

Half year figures showed that Sunderland had a higher shipping tonnage than any other single town or city in the world. The town's light shipyards had produced 245,163 tons.

Six town councillors representing Roker and Seaburn announced a plan of action against what they described as desecration of Seaburn Recreation Park. They suggested that the park should revert to its original purpose of an open space for the benefit of the elderly and the young. The councillors were concerned that there appeared to be a constant stream of events and exhibitions during the summer months and the blaring microphones were a nuisance to residents. One councillor reminded the town council that when the land was transferred to Sunderland Corporation by the Church Commissioners it was on the understanding that it would be used for special events on only a limited number of days each year.

Demolition began on St. Peters Church in Green Street. The seventy year old church closed in 1949 having been declared redundant under the Reorganisation Areas Measure. Prior to 1949 the church served two thousand parishioners who were subsequently taken in by Bishopwearmouth Parish Church.

On 15th August 1951, a television test reception in the Sunderland area revealed that transmission in the test areas of East Herrington, Seaburn and Mile Bank were "steady but poor".

A house in Eston Road behind Fulwell Mill was scheduled for demolition without ever having been completed. The building of the house was started in 1939 but the arrival of war coupled with a shortage of building materials meant that work was halted. The building suffered bomb damage during hostilities and with the sudden rush of post war building work the house was forgotten. By 1951, and with the owner declared bankrupt, the house was deemed to be in an unreasonable state for completion. It was demolished and a bungalow built on the site.

45,000 light bulbs were switched on to herald the start of Roker and Seaburn's biggest ever illuminations. The big switch on was 8th September 1951 and during the thirty day extravaganza some 467,894 people had enjoyed the display.

By the end of 1951 Sunderland's post war building programme stood at 5,153 council houses. The first steps were taken by the corporation's Housing Committee to acquire 169 acres of land at Grindon Farms on which it was proposed to build 1,200 houses on what would become the town's eighth post war housing estate. Work was scheduled to start in 1954.

One of Sunderland's best known landmarks, the blacksmith's shop at the junction of Newcastle Road and Southwick Road, was demolished in December 1951 in accordance with a corporation scheme to widen the approaches to the reconstructed Southwick Road bridge. The shop was believed to have been over two hundred years old at the time.

Above
The blacksmith's shop at the junction of Newcastle Road and Southwick Road.
The shop was demolished in December 1951

1951 was an outstanding year for trade at the Port Of Sunderland with coal shipments at their highest level since 1939. The year saw exports running at their highest level in any peacetime year while imports were the highest recorded in the history of the port.

Right
An idyllic fifties view of Roker Park lake circa 1951.

The Sunderland Echo
and Shipping Gazette

(79th YEAR)
No. 25,047   WEDNESDAY, February 6, 1952.   THREE HALFPENCE

THE KING DIES IN HIS SLEEP

Retired Last Night in Usual Health, Then Passed Away

A PEACEFUL END

BRITAIN, the Commonwealth and Empire join the Royal Family in mourning for King George the Sixth, who died in his sleep early this morning at Sandringham.

King George, who was 57, retired to rest last night in his usual health. He had been out in the grounds during yesterday morning and afternoon, and to everyone he appeared in the very best of health.

Princess Elizabeth became Queen immediately following her father's death. This is the first time in history a British Sovereign has acceded to the Throne while abroad. She, too, becomes Britain's first reigning Queen since the death of her great-great-grandmother, Queen Victoria.

Queen Elizabeth now becomes Queen Mother and Prince Charles is heir to the Throne, with Princess Anne as second in succession. Both children are at Sandringham, where they went on Friday upon their parents' departure on their Commonwealth tour. A question which is unresolved, so far as is known, is the title which the Duke of Edinburgh, Consort to the New Queen, will take.

King George had reigned for 15 years. He ascended the Throne in 1937, following the Abdication of his elder brother, King Edward the Eighth, now the Duke of Windsor.

King George the Sixth will go down in history as a monarch who put duty before everything else—including his own health. Never a man of robust physique, he carried out his onerous duties without regard for his personal safety or well-being.

He was supported throughout his reign by the unwavering help and encouragement of his Queen. They shared the responsibilities and joys of their high position, always showing to the Empire, and the world, a perfect example in their family life.

In 1949 the King underwent an operation known as lumbar sympathectomy to free the flow of blood to his right leg.

He previously had three operations. In 1914, when he was 18, he was put ashore from H.M. battleship Collingwood, in which he was serving, for an appendicitis operation. He rejoined the ship afterwards.

In 1917 he was operated on for duodenal ulcer. A poisoned hand necessitated surgical treatment in 1934.

Narrow Escape in War

In the war the King and Queen escaped death or serious injury when bombs fell on Buckingham Palace in September, 1940.

The King's own account of the raid, quoted by Mr Churchill in the second volume of his war memoirs, states that His Majesty and the Queen had returned to the Palace from Windsor to find an air raid in progress. Going upstairs to a small sitting-room they watched from the window and saw two bombs falling into the Quadrangle.

The blast from the exploding bombs blew in the windows opposite them, and two huge craters appeared in the Quadrangle about 80 yards away.

Fortunately, the sitting-room windows were open at the time; otherwise, as Mr Churchill points out, the whole of the glass might have splintered into the faces of the King and Queen.

The King's Illness

ON May 24 the King was found to be suffering from a mild attack of influenza and confined to his room for a week on the advice of his doctors.

June 1.—Medical bulletin disclosed that "there is now a small area of catarrhal inflammation in the lung, but the constitutional disturbance is slight."

June 4.—Bulletin stated that the inflammation had not entirely disappeared. General condition had improved but complete rest was considered essential. Public engagements cancelled.

Sept. 1.—Dr George Cordiner, the radiologist, and Dr Geoffrey Marshall, the chest specialist, flew to Balmoral where the King was on holiday.

An announcement followed that the King would visit London for an examination.

Sept. 8.—The King travelled by train to London, spent an hour and a half at Dr Cordiner's consulting rooms, and returned by air.

Sept. 11.—It was announced from Buckingham Palace that the King would return to London for treatment.

Sept. 15.—The King flew from Scotland to London.

Sept. 18.—Bulletin signed by nine doctors stated that a series of examinations had been carried out including radiology and bronchoscopy. These "showed structural changes to have developed in the lung." The King was advised to stay in London for further treatment. The Queen flew from Balmoral to London with Princess Elizabeth and the Duke of Edinburgh.

Sept. 21.—Seven doctors decided on operation.

Sept. 23.—Operation performed. Bulletins stated the King's condition continued as satisfactorily as could be expected, but anxiety must remain for some days.

THE *SUNDERLAND ECHO* REPORTED THE DEATH OF
KING GEORGE VI ON 6TH FEBRUARY 1952.

In 1952 ...

Tea rationing ended.

Identity cards were abolished.

The first jet airline service began.

The Mousetrap opened in London's West End.

The first sex change operation was performed.

King George IV died.

The last London tram ran.

Tea bags were first introduced in Britain.

The first heart pacemaker was used.

Flip top cigarette packets were introduced in Britain.

Britain became the world's third nuclear power when it exploded its own test atomic bomb.

Above
Indoore television aerials were a technological breakthrough in the fifties.

Left
A motoring name from the past

In Sunderland in 1952...

When a superstitious housewife discovered that her new house in Dykelands Road was number 13, she wrote to the Corporation and the Borough Engineers Department agreed to change the house number to 12½. At this point it was decided that tenants on future Sunderland housing estates should be protected against "evil spirits" and number thirteen was subsequently ommited from streets of council houses. Newcastle did not share Sunderland's allergy to the sinister number with one Tyneside official commenting, "We're not superstitious like Wearside although I believe there are other towns which share Sunderland's crankiness." The corporation was not the town's sole observer of the ancient fear. The Royal Infirmary and General Hospitals numbered their wards 11,12,14 etc.

By February 1952 the cost of living was starting to rise and according to the *Sunderland Echo* it was even becoming expensive to drown one's sorrows. The comment was made in the light of a 1d increase in the price of a pint of draught beer. The increase meant that the cost of a pint of the cheapest draught beer was 1s 2d (6p) per pint.

For the first time in its history, the future of Thorney Close Hall was considered by Sunderland Corporation. By 1952, the stately 400 year old mansion was lying in the heart of a modern housing estate. Following the death of owner Miss Violet Bulkley, the last surviving link in a long line of descendents, the future of the house which was once set in the beautiful surroundings of a vineyard, had suddenly become uncertain.

Above
Thorney Close Hall awaits its fate in March 1952. For several months the future of the 400 year old building had hung in the balance but when plans to convert it into a workingmen's club fell through, the bulldozers moved in during the following year.

Left
A quiet game of bowls at Roker Park during the spring of 1952.

Venus was blamed for a spate of vandalism in Mowbray Park. The Roman goddess of love was also a former Roman goddess of gardens and one theory was that this had influenced the angry lovers who had torn down saplings and uprooted hedges on the night in question. The park's superintendent commented that the bowling pavilion in Mowbray Park was a well known rendezvous for courting couples and when a number of couples were chased from the premises by park keepers they were seen running in the direction of the newly planted saplings and hedges. "The couples must have taken revenge by destroying the plants," claimed the park's superintendent. Mowbray Park was the most central park and yet the only unlocked park in Sunderland. It was suggested that gates should be fixed to the park to keep out the courting couples and if Sunderland Corporation were unable to finance the project, the superintendent offered to assist with the erection himself! In the meantime he said that he intended taking extra precautions to minimise the problem!!

The shipyard of Joseph L. Thompson & Sons announced an order to construct a 26,450 ton motor ship, the company's biggest ever order. Together with a vessel of similar size which had been ordered from the Deptford shipyard of Sir James Laing & Sons, the ship shared the distinction of being the largest vessel to be built in Wearside's 600 year shipbuilding history.

Police officers raided a social club in Park Lane and arrested the club steward on the charge of keeping the premises as a betting house. During the raid, betting slips, an account book and three tins containing more than £15 were seized.

By April 1952 it seemed as if the 'barrow boy' culture was about to disappear from Sunderland altogether. There were just half a dozen stalls trading with several more lying on their sides at the Victoria Hall bombed site. The *Sunderland Echo* called it a graveyard scene and predicted the demise of street trading in the town unless action was taken. The barrow boys had once numbered forty but were gradually drifting out of business having been moved from one site to another since the turn of the decade. Sites at High Street and Union Street had been recent homes to the traders.

Left
Harry Kirtley,
Sunderland AFC player
of the early fifties.

Right
A peaceful Whitburn village
in October 1952.

Alarm bells were ringing amidst the prediction that Sunderland's population would soon be down by 2,000 as a result of emigration to the Dominions. The exodus from Sunderland caused industrialists and employment organisations to panic as heavy overseas demand for skilled men of all trades threatened to have far reaching effects. Of the recent departures, more than one hundred and fifty people had sailed on a one way trip to Canada through one Sunderland travel agent alone while there was a four year waiting list for Wearsiders wishing to try their luck in New Zealand. Meanwhile, more than two hundred enquiries were taken by an Australian immigration officer on a short visit to the town. Southern Rhodesia was also a popular destination amongst disillusioned town folk. The reasons given for the immigration urge were the weather, a fear of unemployment, better wages and poor housing conditions.

No town in Northern England could boast better shopping facilities than Sunderland. With over 175 shops to serve every ten thousand of its population, the ratio compared favourably with Newcastle, South Shields, Gateshead and other neighbouring areas. The figures were revealed in "Britain's Shop" and was the first survey of its kind to be carried out by the Board Of Trade. The survey showed that there were 40,075 shops in the northern region and this equated to an average of 128 shops per ten thousand people.

There was disheartening news for the ten thousand families on the town's housing waiting list. With just 553 houses built in the first six months of the year, the corporation announced that it would fall well short of its 1952 target of fifteen hundred new houses. The corporation blamed its failure on the cumulative effect of continual shortages of materials and difficulty in locating the necessary labour.

A row broke out between Sunderland Corporation and the British Railways Executive concerning the latter's proposals to carry out a £59,000 renovation job on the south end of Sunderland's central station. The Corporation reluctantly agreed to the proposals, describing them as a patch up job which would fail to provide railway facilities "adequate for and commensurate with a town of the size and importance of Sunderland." It added that the British Railways Executive should give priority to building an entirely new railway station as soon as economic conditions improved. The renovation involved the erection of a new roof, new front and the building of a booking office, bookstall and waiting room.

Left
An interior view of Sunderland's central railwaty station in December 1952.

Right
It's July 1952 and a new single decker bus from the Sunderland District fleet awaits departure from the south end of Sunderland's central railway station. The station was modernised shortly after this photograph was taken.

Above
Strawberry Farm Cottage in June 1952.
Strawberries and cream were once served to the public from the gardens of the property.

The shipbuilding output in Sunderland was the lowest for thirteen years, despite the fact that there were more orders on the books than at any time in the past. An acute steel shortage and delays in allocated supplies had seriously disrupted production but assurances had been given to the shipbuilding industry by the Admiralty that nine per cent more steel would be made available in the first quarter of 1953 than was allocated in the fourth quarter of 1952.

Sunderland Corporation Seaside Development Committee's decision to allow Sunday night dancing at Seaburn Hall was attacked by the Sunderland Free Church Council as being "another step towards the continental Sunday."

Coal shipments from the Port Of Sunderland were 3,189,000 tons and were the highest since 1939. The figure represented an increase of 446,000 tons on 1951. Although coal exports were steadily increasing, a NCB spokesman said that it would be a long time before Sunderland returned to the days when it exported two million tons per year.

For three minutes, two men stood talking in the middle of a zebra crossing at the junction of Ryhope Road and Mowbray Road and held up a line of traffic. They ignored a request from a policeman to move and were arrested for "failing to go over a pedestrian crossing with reasonable dispatch." In the first trial of its kind in the area, Sunderland Magistrates were told by the men that they were only talking and were doing no harm. The Magistrate laid down that "the pedestrian has certain things to observe and one of them is that he should not loiter."

An Admiralty order for small minesweepers was placed with a Sunderland shipyard. It was one of the first naval peacetime contracts to be allocated to the Wear. It had long been the contention of Sunderland shipbuilders that facilities existed on the Wear for such peacetime work but they had nevertheless constantly been overlooked.

Having made shipbuilding history in 1951 when it launched two half ships, the yard of John Crown & Sons secured a second order to build a ship by that method. The order was for a 18,250 ton tanker for a customer in Bergen, Norway. The previous order had been for a 23,000 ton motor tanker for Oslo and it was revealed that in the vessel's wardroom were two half crowns in a glass case which were given by the Crown yard's workforce as a permanent reminder of the name given by them to the ship, "the half crown ship".

Left
The crowds flocked to see The Centurion *in dock during September 1952.*

Right
Greenwell's dry dock in September 1952.

Sunderland Corporation had been wasteful with the land which it had acquired for past developments and should not be trusted in the future according to a solicitor speaking on behalf of C. Vaux & Sons at a public enquiry into the compulsory purchase of 250 acres of land at Grindon. The solicitor described the Corporation as "this sprawling octopus" and said since 1945 it had acquired 1133 acres of good farm land by compulsory purchase alone and of the six post war compulsory purchase applications it had won them all. Of the land at Grindon, he said that it was excellent for farming and cows raised on it had produced prize winning milk yields. The solicitor concluded that there was little point in farmers working hard in their drive for national food production if this fearful monster (the Corporation) was going to come down on them at anytime.

Residents in Silver Street reported that they were dreading the onset of winter as they lived in fear of high winds and heavy rain bringing down the tarpaulin covered roofs of their homes. For seven years they had endured dreadful living conditions in the war damaged properties and their plight was highlighted by one resident who said, "My home is falling around me. We have crumbling roofs, damaged ceilings and ruined furniture. When it rains, the bedroom floor is covered with water."

Barrack Bungalows in Barrack Street were 21 years old in October. When they were built in 1931, the neat row of twelve wooden houses overlooking the South Docks were intended as temporary accommodation for no longer than five years. The tenants had moved into the Barrack Bungalows from their former homes in North Moor Street which were being demolished to make way for the construction of a deep water quay. The *Sunderland Echo* greeted the bungalows' coming of age with a mixture of surprise and pleasure; surprise that they were still standing sixteen years after they were supposed to have been pulled down and pleasure that they were as sturdy and cosy as ever. The bungalows were unique to Sunderland and according to residents they were a big improvement on their homes in North Moor Street as they had hot and cold water as well as bathrooms inside the house.

It was revealed that drunkeness was on the increase in Sunderland. The number of people proceeded against by the police during the year was 135 compared with 129 in 1952. The figure was the highest in the town for ten years. However, Sunderland's record compared favourably with other towns and in a national survey of twenty three towns Sunderland finished fourth lowest.

Left
This photograph was taken by the Sunderland Echo in 1952 to illustrate the new traffic signs of the day. Two way traffic in Fawcett Street was the norm and head scarves were seemingly very fashionable.

Right
A Sunderland Corporation tram and a Northern General bus at Ryhope Road circa 1952.

The Sunderland Echo
and Shipping Gazette

(80th YEAR)

No. 25,487   TUESDAY, July 7, 1953.   THREE HALFPENCE

COMMERCIAL TV: NORTH-EAST PLANS

Five Applications Affect Durham

By Our Lobby Correspondent

FIVE applications have so far been made for licences for commercial television stations in the coastal area between Sunderland and the Hartlepools. Four are for high-power transmitters and one for a low-power station.

This information is given in the first report of the Television Advisory Committee, published to-day. The names of the applicants are not disclosed.

The Committee sent a questionnaire to applicants for competitive T.V. transmitter licences and rather more than half of the replies gave details of transmitter requirements and preferred frequency bands—H.F. (very high frequency) or U.H.F. (ultra high frequency). Six applicants plan coverage of all the main population centres of the country.

The replies received disclose applications for 88 transmitters which may represent a total at present of about 150 or 160 transmitters applied for. Of the 67 applications are for high-power stations, eight for medium power and 13 for low power.

Fifteen applicants cluster in London and Home Counties area. Manchester and West Riding applicants so far want stations and in the Birmingham area there are applications for eight stations.

There are three applications for high-power stations in Cumberland and one in North Northumberland.

Difficulties

If the report does nothing else it underlines the tremendous technical difficulties ahead of the sponsored TV controversy irrespective of the political and social issues.

It is a question of room in the air for all the frequencies which may eventually be required. In a reservation report one of the committee, Dr C. O. Stanley (Radio Industry Council) refers to the present chaotic condition" of frequency allocation.

The B.B.C. wants all the H.F. room at present available for completion of its national coverage and the establishment in its ten-year programme of a country-wide second TV programme with regional bias.

If the B.B.C. gets what it wants it would mean that only the ultra high frequency wave bands would be left for the sponsored TV operators, with greater expense to achieve wide coverage of any given area.

Referring to the available H.F. wavelengths the report says: "Clearly, they cannot provide both a complete second B.C. programme and a coverage of extensive areas by competitive television. One or the other, or both, must suffer."

This gives point to the safeguards roughly sketched in last week's Government statement. It could be suggested that the Government, that the number of sponsored TV stations would be limited in number, of low power, and limited range. The advisory Committee suggests that a few such stations in remote parts of the country could be squeezed in among the big fellows in the V.H.F. waveband.

MAJOR "NOT INVOLVED IN HOLD-UP"

A self-confessed Corsican gangster, Barthelemy Ruberti, told a crowded court at Aix-en-Provence to-day that Major Lindsay Watson, Anglo-French hero of two world wars, had no part in the robbery of the Begum Aga Khan's jewels, valued at £200,000. Watson is among those facing charges arising from the hold-up of the Begum, former French beauty queen, in a daring daylight coup four years ago. He is accused of aiding and abetting a typhoon lashed the Korean and receiving stolen goods.

The beautiful Begum, in a smart yellow costume, was in court to-day. Ruberti, one of the accused men, said in reply to Judge Vahan Portoukalran, that he was one of the five men who held up the Aga Khan's car on the lonely Cannes-Nice road on August 3, 1949. He declared: "I regret to see Watson in the accused box. He is not the major who was involved in this affair."

DISNEYS HERE.—Smiles round the door from Hollywood film producer Walt Disney and his wife on their arrival at Southampton from New York in the Cunard liner Queen Elizabeth.   —Picture by Wire.

TYPHOON THREAT AS BATTLE RAGES

AFTER a night of fierce hand-to-hand fighting in knee-deep mud a battle still raged on the Korean West Central front to-day.

More than 2,000 Chinese troops were flung against Allied defences as the fringe of a typhoon lashed the Korean battleline, the Eighth Army reported.

Torrential rain, flooding rivers and curtailing Allied air operations, fell on Korea yesterday in the wake of the typhoon which swept into West Korea from the Yellow Sea.

The typhoon is expected to pass over Pyongyang, the North Korean capital, and may cause serious damage to Communist supply lines — many of their bridges are flimsy temporary wooden structures.

Miners May Not Make Claim For All-Round Increase

THE conference of the National Union of Mineworkers at Hastings to-day went into private session to discuss its future wage policy.

The conference sat in private session for nearly two hours considering wages policy and then adjourned until this afternono. So many delegates wanted to speak on the subject that the timetable was varied.

It is understood that the Kent resolution asking for a substantial increase for all miners was withdrawn in favour of the Scottish one asking for an increase for day-wage men. This means that whatever decision is taken later, an all-round increase for all workers in the industry will not be pursued.

Before going into private session delegates heard a fraternal address by Mr Tom O'Brien, M.P., Chairman of the T.U.C. Council.

He said that to read and hear some people within their own movement and people who from time to time "had a go" at trade union leaders, one would imagine that the vast British trade union movement was merely a glorified industrial committee of the Labour Party.

Railmen's Leader Warns

WE SHALL FIGHT IF NECESSARY

NATIONAL Union of Railwaymen delegates in conference at Paignton, Devon, to-day heard their General Secretary, Mr James H. Campbell, say: "I give the warning that this great organization of transport workers is not going to allow its membership to sink into the abyss which might be created as a result of unscrupulous competition."

Mr Campbell was speaking on a three-part resolution—unanimously accepted—which welcomed the Labour Party's assurance that it will re-nationalize transport, called for the greater participation by workers in management and control of nationalized transport, and promised every means to prevent any deterioration in the industry or any worsening of living standards and conditions for members arising from the Transport Bill.

Mr Campbell described the new Transport Bill as discriminatory legislation by the Conservative Government, which was bound to affect railwaymen.

"Humanity is the most precious possession we have, and in the protection of humanity we, as a labour movement and a trade union movement, must make it the pre-eminent matter.

"HAVE THE RIGHT"

"If it is necessary, we should fight, not only to protect our interests, but to improve them, and as an industrial organization we retain the right to do so.

"If conditions are worsened by discriminatory legislation, we have the right, as an industrial organization, to oppose it and to fight it."

If there were to be changes, they had to be faced, and so long as these changes gave protection and reasonable conditions to the people they represented, they would accept the resolution, declared: "No one need get the wind up, as no one need feel we shall indulge in industrial action except as a last resort."

The Lioness Was As Jealous As a Cat

A LION-TAMER, David Togni, entered the lions' cage of a circus at Naples, Italy, last night when a furious fight broke out between a jealous lioness and her mate just after the show. He could not separate the maddened beasts and when the fight was over he had to shoot the dying lioness, Brscia.

She had attacked Pasha, the lord of the lion's cage, because of his attentions to a new arrival a sleek, beautiful lioness named Messalina.

"We cannot have that. The British trade union movement created the Labour Party and if the child thinks it is going to devour the father then the child must be told there is nothing doing.

"Whatever party is in power, whatever may be the difficulties on the political side, the trade union movement must remain free, unfettered and independent and proceed with its own work in protecting its members in every industry.

"We must not deport from that principle which is not incompatible with our loyalty to the Party we created or to our desire and determination that the Party returned to power.

CONSULTATION

"We must ourselves deal with our own problems in our own way and continue constructive consultation with the Labour Party on all great matters affecting the country and affecting industry."

He asked: "Are we to cease representing the day to day work of our people merely because there is a government in power we do not like?

"We must get our thinking clear. Democracy is the first essential principle and it is on

Continued in Back Page

FIVE APPLICATIONS WERE RECEIVED FROM WOULD-BE LICENCEES FOR THE NORTH EAST BASED COMMERCIAL TELEVISION FRANCHISE.

27

In 1953 ...

The Korean War ended.

Marilyn Monroe shocked the world when she posed nude for a calendar.

Polio vaccine was introduced.

A typical three bedroomed semi detached house cost £2000.

England won The Ashes for the first time in twenty years.

Dylan Thomas died.

280 people perished in a storm on England's east coast.

Mount Everest was conquered.

England lost to Hungary in their first post war defeat at Wembley.

British television ownership rose to 3 million.

Casino Royale became the first published James Bond novel.

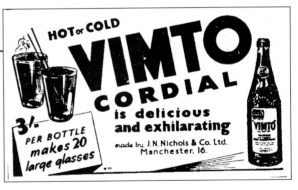

Above
Vimto for less than 2d per glass.

Above
Books Fashions whose services included moth proofing.

Left
Sunderland's own sauce at a bargain price.

In Sunderland in 1953...

In January, the Bristol Aircraft Company at Pallion Trading Estate opened an extension to its number two factory and created work for an extra 250 men. The extension was opened to satisfy worldwide demand for the company's aeroplane engine component parts and the new factory brought the site's total workforce up to one thousand. The Bristol Aircraft Company first came to Sunderland in November 1951 when it took over the former Sunex factory with a workforce of 250. It subsequently doubled the number of employees upon extending into the old Mayfair Cabinet Works premises. The success story then continued with the introduction of a night shift and the creation of a further 250 jobs.

Sunderland AFC created a new football record when the largest travelling cup tie crowd in the club's history - ten thousand fans - made a mass exodus to Burnley. Officials described the rush for tickets as "staggering" as seven thousand supporters booked their seats on a special convoy of trains which left Sunderland at fifteen minute intervals. The previous record for travelling supporters was the seven thousand who travelled to London for the cup tie with Tottenham Hotspur in January 1950.

Plans were announced for the biggest private house development in Sunderland for thirteen years when Sunderland Corporation Planning & Highways Committee approved the layout for a seven hundred housing estate in the Dene Lane/Shields Road area of town. Planning permission was also given for a private undertaking of fifty houses on Mere Knolls estate. At the time, the *Sunderland Echo* reported that the average cost of houses being built privately had risen to £2,000 which was almost four times the cost of a similar type of house in 1939.

Above
This Christmas card scene captures a snow blizzard at Bridge Street during the winter of 1952/1953, when Boydells was the place to shop for cycles and all sorts of toys.

The Circle tram route was scrapped by Sunderland Corporation Transport as buses took over. The cost of the reinstatement of roads involved three sections of route; Kayll Road to Summerhill, Kayll Road to Trimdon Street and Trimdon Street to Fawcett Street at a total cost of £77,460. Thirty buses were ordered for the servicing of the route and at this point only thirty nine trams remained in the Sunderland fleet. This included tramcar number 100 which at 40 feet long (compared to the standard length of 30 feet) and with a capacity for 70 passengers (compared to the standard 58), it was the largest of its type in the country. The vehicle was ultimately purchased for £100 by a group of preservation enthusiasts.

Building started on the town's seventh post war housing estate at Castletown where it was proposed to build 1,750 houses. A total expenditure of £2½ million was allocated to the 1953/1954 council budget for house building and site preparations. It was revealed that Sunderland had the best record in the north east for post war house building, according to figures issued by the Ministry Of Housing & Local Government. By December 1952, 8,116 houses had been built in Sunderland compared with Newcastle who fared next best with 6,482.

Above
A tranquil view of Low Quay, Sunderland in July 1953.

In January, Sunderland town council signed an entente cordiale with French seaport town St. Nazaire in an attempt to foster friendly relations between two towns with so much in common. St. Nazaire was described as the largest shipbuilding centre in France with other principal industries including aircraft construction, ship repair and steel making.

Above
A tram passes the recently re-opened Binns store at Fawcett Street in 1953.

In February, three floors of the largest departmental store in northern England welcomed its first customers when Binns' new store opened. The store took three years to build and its opening filled a twelve year gap in Sunderland's shopping life. The original store which stood on the site was razed by German bombs on 10th April 1941.

Sunderland's first two national trade conferences were staged. The National Federation Of Fish Friers brought four hundred delegates to the town while one hundred and fifty delegates converged on Sunderland from the Association Of Sea & Airport Authorities.

Sunderland Corporation's Seaside Development Committee reported disappointing financial results relating to the 1952 season of illuminations. The cost of staging the event was £8,000 cheaper than for the previous year and it had been expected to recoup all running costs from admission charges to Roker Park. The deficit was met by adding 1/2d to the rates. The committee reported that heavy rain during the illuminations season had limited the total attendance at Roker Park to 228,337 (compared with 472,253 in 1951) which accounted for receipts of £9,859. In announcing the 1953 Coronation Lights, the Seaside Development Committee recommended the town council to agree a four week programme of illuminations at an estimated cost of £18,125; an increase of £6,025 on the previous year.

The *Sunderland Echo* highlighted the problems of living in Pennywell, given the fact that it was an outpost in the town. The reporter mentioned that when Pennywell estate was built in 1947, it was actually situated outside the County Borough boundary. Subsequent boundary extensions made the estate a member of the town's sturdy family of post war houses although Pennywell retained the unenviable distinction of being further from the centre of Sunderland than any other estate. The *Sunderland Echo* said that Pennywell's geographical position coloured the lives of the housewives, workmen and children who lived there and it was so far out of town that it had the novel aspect of being an English country village without a past. The earliest families to move to Pennywell found themselves face to face with countryside once described as "the town without its clothes on".

Alarmed at the low morals of many young girls in Sunderland, the Standing Conference Of Women's Organisations which represented 15,000 women on Wearside agreed that more policewomen were needed in the town. They were quoted as saying that they deplored the behaviour of a number of fourteen to eighteen year old girls who were associating with seamen in the town's dockland area. The organisation called for quick and decisive action, claiming that Sunderland ranked as one of the north's blackspots for prostitution. The alleged trouble was confined to foreign ships docking in Sunderland whereupon it was quite common for girls to stay on board over the weekend. Chief Constable for the police said that a close watch was being kept on the docks and that the problems generally arose when girls followed ships down the coast or travelled on them. He said that the value of more policewomen, where they were required to go aboard the ships and confront drunken sailors, was small and that the job should be one for a man.

It was decided to market Seaburn as a 'short holiday resort' following a report presented by Sunderland Corporation Entertainments Committee. It was decided to advertise Seaburn by displaying hundreds of pictorial posters at selected railway stations throughout the north of England. A distinct lack of accommodation in the area was given as the main reason against marketing Seaburn as a long term holiday resort.

Above
340 lightbulbs decorated this Sunderland Corporation bus as part of the 1953 Coronation celebrations. It is seen here at the town's Fulwell Depot.

A 71 year old grandmother appeared in court for the forty fourth time charged with theft. She first appeared in the courts as a fifteen year old in 1897 and had indulged in thieving for most of her life. The grey haired pensioner was spotted in a Fawcett Street store not attempting to buy anything but engaged in burrowing her way into crowds of shoppers in congested areas of the store. A policewomen followed her into the railway station where she struck up a conversation with the suspect before noticing three purses in a shopping bag, one of which answered the description of a stolen item. A Chief Inspector commented, "I don't think I've seen a criminal record like this one ever before." The woman had served forty two previous prison sentences.

A seven year plan was announced to bring electricity into 118,000 north east homes, including almost 6000 in the Wearside area. The North Eastern Electricity Consultative Council estimated the cost of the work to be £6,400,000 and said that the plan had resulted from numerous requests for electricity being presented to the Board. The first stage of the work would benefit five hundred people in Sunderland.

Plans were announced by Sunderland Corporation Transport Committee to operate a 'one man - one bus' service on the Hill View route. The proposals meant that bus drivers on the route would also become conductors. Transport manager Mr. Norman Morton said that the recent extension to the Leechmere Road route had resulted in a loss of passengers on the Hill View service but as it had been running since 1937, he felt that it was unreasonable to withdraw it. The loss of revenue would be partially offset by the introduction of one man operation. To assist the driver, passengers would be encouraged to buy books of pre-booked tickets at preferential rates. The four single deck buses in the corporation fleet would be converted to one man operation if the proposals were accepted.

Above
Scaffolding surrounds the Kings Theatre on a quiet day in Crowtree Road during 1953.
The name Hugh Mitchell will be remembered with fondness as one of the town's main shoe retailers at that time.

Above
Ryhope Hall in May 1953.

A deputation of television viewers from the Roker area complained to the town council about interference on their sets caused by an illumination set piece in Roker Park. The residents complained strongly that the council refused to fit suppressors to the offending set piece 'Feeding Time For Fledglings'. Elsewhere, Sunderland people continued to support the illuminations with over 50,000 patrons visiting Roker Park in a typical week. The spectacle was described as being "better and brighter than Blackpool" by Sunderland's entertainments manager.

Work began on the construction of the then biggest ship to be built on the River Wear. The ship was the 26,000 ton Fleet Auxiliary oil tanker which, upon completion at Sir James Laing & Sons of Deptford, became one of the biggest in the entire Royal Fleet Auxiliary with greater speed capabilities than other ships in the fleet. The ship had a length of 583 feet and a beam of 71 feet.

The Hendon factory of Prices Tailors Ltd. closed down on 27th November when it put one thousand girls out of work. The ultra modern factory in Commercial Road was government built under the control of the North Eastern Trading Estates Ltd. and was leased to Prices in 1947. Meanwhile, the town's confectionery company Mayfair Products Ltd. announced the likelihood of three hundred new jobs following their acquisition of the Grangetown premises of the former Robinson's cabinet making works. Mayfair Products took over sweet manufacturing in Sunderland during 1943 and increased demand for their confectionery necessitated the purchase of the Grangetown site for expansion. A company spokesman said, "Although most of the Prices workforce had been machinists, they would be able to quickly adapt themselves to sweet factory work."

Above

A row of houses at Silver Street in 1953 with their tarpaulin covered roofs which had been intended as temporary repairs following war damage in 1945.

Above

The scene is the north end of Sunderland's railway station in 1953 but the reason for the queue is unclear.

Above
The south end of Sunderland's central railway station is seen here following modernisation in 1953.

The agent and secretary of Sunderland Borough Labour Party speaking at the party conference in Margate asked the conference to amend the executive's plan for the industry which was to set up a development council on which both shipbuilding and engineering would be represented. In pledging that the industry should be placed under public ownership, Mr. Geoffrey Foster said, "We are particularly conscious of the 25,000 unemployed which existed in Sunderland during the thirties which was due to a slump suffered by the shipbuilding industry. We do not believe that private enterprise could cure this disease if it occurred again as we are concerned by the failures of the industry's present owners." He continued to say that under private enterprise the cost of British marine products was likely to rise and be higher than that of foreign competition. This, he predicted, would result in mass unemployment in Sunderland's shipyards.

The government announced a proposal to re-start the country's slum clearance programme which had been suspended upon the declaration of war. Only one major slum clearance had been undertaken in Sunderland since 1939, Low Pallion where two hundred houses had been demolished to make way for the extensions to the engine works of William Doxford & Sons. Under the banner of "Operation Rescue" the Corporation was able to proceed with the demolition of 120 houses in the Lawrence Street, Hendon Road and the Commercial Road areas. The corporation announced its subsequent intentions to build multi-storey flats to accommodate 300 families.

Left
*A breathtaking view of the
River Wear taken from
Corporation Quay in 1953.*

Sunderland experienced its best shipbuilding output since the war. Thanks to a last minute spate of orders, the annual tonnage soared to 199,254 tons which was accounted for 27 1/2 ships. The half ship was represented by the first section of a tanker which was launched from the yard of John Crown.

Site preparation was completed for the construction of Sunderland's eighth post war housing estate at Grindon Village and tenders were invited for the initial building of 277 council houses. The eventual number of houses at Grindon Village was expected to be 1,200 with many catering for smaller families. At this point, Sunderland's record for post war house construction was Springwell (822 houses), Thorney Close (1,689), Hillview (528), Pennywell (2,358), Hylton Red House (1,044), Farringdon (1,800), Castletown (1,750) and Grindon Village (1,200). The ninth estate on the drawing board was an extension to Hylton Red House.

A season of 'Know The Town' tours were run by Sunderland Corporation Transport as part of the Coronation celebrations. The purpose of the bus trips was to show Sunderland townspeople the Coronation decorations and also give people the chance to see the new housing estates and to show them how Sunderland had grown in post war years.

Above
Sunderland's main post office at Sunniside in 1953.

ROTARY WATCHES

WALKERS THE MODERN JEWELLERS SUNDERLAND

The Sunderland Echo
and Shipping Gazette

(81st YEAR)

No. 25,935   TUESDAY, December 14, 1954.   THREE HALFPENCE

County Final

FIRE WRECKS TOWN STORE

Damage Exceeds £1,000,000

SUNDERLAND'S worst fire of the century destroyed the four-story departmental store of Joplings in High Street West early to-day. It is estimated that damage will amount to more than £1 million. No one was injured.

Much of the property surrounding the store was badly damaged and squads of men were to-day clearing up debris from the streets. Firemen are still pouring water into the shell of the store at the rate of 1,200 gallons a minute. It will be noon to-morrow before the hoses can be turned off because the remains of the building are still hot and there is a danger that fire might break out again.

Chief Fire Officer T. Bruce said this afternoon: "At the height of the fire we were using 3,800 gallons of water a minute from 19 jets. It is a blessing that there was no wind at the time."

After consultations between Corporation officials, the police and fire brigade it was decided to pull down the remains of the store to-morrow.

Other stores in Sunderland are doing their best to help Joplings and are accepting their token money.

MORE PICTURES and the full story of the fire appear in Pages 7, 8, 9 and 10.

ABOVE: The scene in High Street West, Sunderland, early to-day as firemen fought the blaze which destroyed the four-story departmental store of Joplings. Girders twisted in the heat of the town's worst fire of the century, and much of the surrounding property was damaged. BELOW: When daylight came squads of men began to clear the streets of debris. Masses of masonry which had crashed down from a height of 70 feet lay in the road.

A MAJOR FIRE COMPLETELY DESTROYED JOPLINGS' DEPARTMENT STORE IN
HIGH STREET WEST DURING THE EARLY HOURS OF 14TH DECEMBER 1954.

In 1954 ...

Television's first soap opera was transmitted when The Grove Family hit the screens.

All forms of rationing finally ended after fourteen years.

The cost of a television licence increased from £2 to £3.

Oral contraceptives were first tested.

The board game Scrabble first went on sale.

The equivalent of VAT was introduced in France.

Billy Graham toured England.

Roger Bannister broke the four minute mile.

Britain's first purpose built comprehensive school was opened.

Germany won the World Cup.

The first pre-recorded audio tapes went on sale.

Britain's crime rate fell to its lowest post war figure.

Above
Locally produced confectionery from Mayfair.

Right
Oxydol was a detergent brand name which disappeared during the sixties.

In Sunderland in 1954...

Above
One of five double deck buses to be built at Sunderland in 1954. No. 168 in the Sunderland Corporation fleet is seen here undergoing a Ministry of Transport safety test prior to entering passenger service. The bus was built at Southwick by Associated Coachbuilders.

A total of 8,659 Sunderland residents were classified as living in slum conditions.

The first of five double decker buses to be built in Sunderland joined the corporation fleet. The buses were built at the Southwick works of Associated Coachbuilders and the first vehicle entered service on 19th January 1954.

Four hundred people packed into St. Peter's Church Hall in Green Street on 2nd February 1954 to register a strongly worded protest at Sunderland Town Council's plans to continue with the seaside illuminations. The meeting had been arranged by a group of Sunderland ratepayers under the name of the "Anti Illuminations Group" who expressed the view that the illumination events should contribute to the rates rather than cost the ratepayers. In announcing an ambitious campaign, the group announced its intention to canvas every house in Sunderland with the aim of securing 40,000 signatures asking the council to "rid the town of the illuminations".

When a gas meter inspector visited a house in East Street he expected to collect £4 4s 11d but instead he found just 1d. When questioned, the tenant of the house admitted to kicking the lock on the meter door whereupon it came open. "It must have been a poor lock," he said. The tenant admitted to using the same penny time and time again but when it was explained in court that once a 1d dropped into the meter it became the property of the Northern Gas Board and, as such, the accused could be charged with stealing the same penny on 1,018 occasions, the accused's defence commented that it was difficult to prove beyond reasonable doubt that the same penny had been used. The tenant was ordered to repay £4 4s 10d.

By March, a total of 15,328 Sunderland residents had said "no" to the seafront illuminations by signing the petition organised by the Anti Illuminations Group. A spokesman for the group said that the figure had been achieved despite the fact that canvassing had yet to begin in the Pennywell, Red House and Humbledon areas of the town. The group had hoped to present the petition at the April meeting of Sunderland Town Council. However, the council refused to receive the deputation amid jeers of "It's a disgrace" and "a perfect example of democracy" although a promise was made to address the matter at the June meeting.

Left
A major fifties/sixties tourist attraction
was the miniature railway at Seaburn.

Right
Roker old lighthouse in 1954.

General manager of the Sunderland division of the Northern Gas Board said he hoped that the time would not be too distant when smokeless zones were introduced into the town. He said that a practical approach to the smoke abatement problem was long overdue and that it was a great pity that attractive new housing estates had been developed in Sunderland without making some restrictions on the use of coal in the open grate. Meanwhile, the town clerk said that the town of Sunderland needed to be beautified and that it was up to the citizens of the town to make sure that it was done. He suggested that the use of smokeless fuels would reduce the smoke and grime and he called upon the spirit which had built up north east industry to its present dominance to help solve the problems of improving the town's appearance. In launching the 'Our Town' campaign, the town clerk commented, "We have got to recognise the fact that we are an industrial town but at least we can replace the drabness with colour, the ugliness with beauty and smoke with fresh air." He said that it was wrong to think that everything must be done by the council and that it required an effort by every individual as it was everyone's responsibility.

Trams were withdrawn from the Durham Road to Town route on 29th March. At this point only twenty eight trams remained in the Sunderland fleet with only the Fawcett Street to Dykelands Road route awaiting conversion to buses. The section of Durham Road tram track had been laid as recently as 1947. A spokesman for the transport committee said that Sunderland was operating a fleet of mostly secondhand trams which had been purchased from eight towns as they had scrapped their fleets. He said that it would cost more money to update the tram fleet and track than it would to replace the trams with double decker buses. The problem was intensified by the rapid growth of new housing estates on the edge of the Sunderland boundary. He said that the cost of laying one mile of track was £60,000 and that fifteen modern buses could be purchased for the same sum of money.

Sunderland made history on 24th May when it became the first county borough in the country to elect a female mayor and deputy mayor.

Sunderland could boast the cleanest buses in Britain thanks to the installation of a revolutionary giant bus wash machine at the transport department's Hylton Road Depot which was converted to house sixty buses. It was formerly the town's tram depot.

A 61 year old Sunderland man appeared in Sunderland Magistrates Court as a result of using abusive language in his own home. The man from Westheath Avenue told magistrates, "I can swear in my own house if I want to," but the Clerk Of The Court advised him that if he used obscene language in his house and his words could be heard by people outside who were offended as a result, he was then guilty of an offence. A police constable giving evidence told the court that, when asked to come to the door, the man swore at the top of his voice out of the bedroom window. The accused said that the policeman's story was untrue saying, "I did not leave my bed. May I drop stone dead now if I am lying." The Magistrate replied, "Don't do that. It would be most inconvenient."

Above
This 1954 traffic scene in a majestic Fawcett Street captures Sunderland Corporation buses and a tram as well as town centre cyclists and period cars, one of which prepares to turn left into Borough Road.

Sunderland Corporation Estates Committee decided to scrap four hundred American style prefabs at Grindon and Southwick. The prefabs which had been erected in 1946 were found to be in very poor condition and were a constant drain upon the resources of the corporation's maintenance staff. The prefabs were unsuited to the rigours of north east weather and several tenants had complained of ill health caused by dampness in their homes.

In April 1954, council houses in Sunderland were built at a rate of four per day. Of the 130 built during the month, 125 were at Hylton Castle and 5 at Farringdon. In addition, 632 houses were under construction at Hylton Castle and 428 at Grindon, employing a workforce of over seven hundred.

The *Sunderland Echo* of 3rd June reported that Strawberry Cottage - one of the most picturesque reminders of old Sunderland - was set for demolition to make way for a new estate of 150 houses at Strawberry Farm. The cottage got its name because passers-by on their way to Tunstall Hill were served with strawberries and cream in the shady gardens of the property. At one time, beer was also served in the garden. The cottage, which was 150 years old, was solidly built with some walls two feet thick and originally belonged to Doctor Stephen Pemberton who gave it to his daughter Annabella when she married Thomas Wilkinson in 1814.

Above
Union Street bus station in May 1954 with a clear view of the clock tower at the north end of the central railway station. The corporation bus on the left of the photograph was painted in the then familiar red and cream livery while the one on the right sported the newly introduced green and cream colours.

Right
Little has changed in Chester Road since this photograph was taken in 1954.

Above
Prefabs at Nookside built as a wartime measure were unable to tolerate north east weather conditions and were demolished during 1953/1954.

It was announced that Fulwell bus depot was to acquire its own gas cooker in the rest room. The Corporation Transport Committee took the decision when it was reported that the present arrangement of heating food in a tin container on a coke stove was proving to be unsatisfactory. "The situation has been aggravated as the depot cat has taken to sleeping in the container," the committee was told by one member.

Sunderland Meat Mart returned to the town for the first time since the introduction of meat rationing in 1939. One butcher said, "It is great to have the chance of choosing our own meat instead of taking what the Government sends us." After examining the beasts in the pens at the mart in Roker Avenue, butchers began bidding briskly for the 33 cattle and 47 pigs.

A Castletown grave digger was enjoying a peaceful holiday with his wife and eleven children when Hylton Parish Council asked him to dig a grave. He refused to do the job and was immediately sacked and told to quit his cemetery cottage. The work was subsequently carried out by three workmen from Sunderland Rural District Council while the sacked man, who had worked at the cemetery for 27 years, told the *Sunderland Echo*, "I think I was justified in declining the work considering it was my holidays." The man's wife began a petition protesting about the council's action which over seven hundred people signed. The Clerk of the Council subsequently announced that the termination of employment had been withdrawn.

Sunderland Technical College students' rag magazine was banned by the college's principal as it contained too many references to sex. Thousands of copies of the 96 page magazine were on sale throughout County Durham and were withdrawn at a cost of £250 to the students union.

The chairman of the Bishopwearmouth Choral Society told its members assembled at the annual meeting that the temptation of 'knob twisting' was a real enemy to the cause of amateur musical organisations. He said that wartime hostilities had brought with it an interest in music making as a form of self entertainment but this had been short lived due to the opposition of television. However, he was confident that the temptation of 'knob twisting' would not suppress the activities of music making organisations.

In its edition of 15th June, the *Sunderland Echo* reported that it would only be a matter of months before Wearsiders would be able to dial Newcastle telephone numbers directly. Sunderland's acting head postmaster revealed that the post office was soon to install a multi-metering system which would enable subscribers to dial numbers to almost every telephone exchange within a fifteen mile radius.

An extraordinary general meeting of shareholders of S.P. Austin & Sons held on 15th July approved proposals for the merger of the Wear dockyard with the Southwick based shipyard of Wm. Pickersgill & Sons. The Austin site would henceforth be used exclusively for ship repair work while future shipbuilding would be undertaken at Southwick. The companies were two of the oldest shipbuilding concerns on the River Wear. The business of S.P. Austin & Sons dated back to 1826 when shipbuilding was undertaken at North Sands before the company moved to its latter day site in 1846. Wm. Pickersgill & Sons was founded in 1846 and in the days of sailing ships, the yard had a strong reputation as builders of steel barques. In recent years, Austins had been mainly involved with the production of colliers and coasters while Pickersgills had concentrated on the building of high class cargo passenger vessels. The two companies were formally merged on 9th September.

Above
The Theatre Tavern in Lambton Street. The pub opened in the 1850's at the same time as the Lyceum Theatre from which it took its name.

Ambitious plans were announced for a new municipal theatre with accommodation for 1,750 people to be built at Mowbray Park. Subject to approval by the Corporation Parks Committee, plans involved the draining of the Mowbray Park lake prior to building the theatre on the site. Provision was to be made for cars to drive from Burdon Road to the main entrance of the theatre while parking facilities were planned for the Murton Street area. The plans were a scaled down version of original proposals for a 2,000-3,000 capacity theatre with an adjacent 'little theatre' seating 500-600 and a large hall intended for conferences and sporting activities such as boxing. The latter plans were revised as many of the facilities existed elsewhere in the town such as at Seaburn Hall. The intended new municipal theatre would have replaced Sunderland's former mini theatre, the Victoria Hall, which was destroyed by a land mine during the second world war.

Despite the well documented petition against the annual seafront illuminations, Sunderland's Entertainments & Seaside Development Committee ruled that the 1954 events would go ahead as planned. The reason given for the apparent rejection of the petition which had been signed by 24,000 ratepayers was that preparations were too advanced to even contemplate abandonment. The committee agreed to address the various points raised in the objections before plans were made for the 1955 events.

A crowd of 100,000 people - the biggest ever seen in Fawcett Street - welcomed the Queen and Duke of Edinburgh to Sunderland on 29th October. As the Royal couple arrived at the Town Hall entrance, the crowd began chanting "We want the Queen". Eventually, a corporation official unfastened the Town Hall windows and the Royal couple stepped on to the balcony and for several minutes they waved to the cheering crowd of people below.

Above
Corporation transport workmen at the Wheatsheaf depot put the finishing touches to Sunderland's 'Ghost Tram' prior to its final run on 1st October 1954.

Above
Council dignatories board the last ever tram to run in Sunderland on 1st October 1954.

1st October 1954 was a day of great sadness for many Wearsiders. It was the day on which the last tram clanked its way through the streets of Sunderland. At 11.20pm, a procession of six trams left the Town Hall for Seaburn and then returned to the Wheatsheaf depot on a special journey which cost members of the public 1/- each for this last and historic ride which brought to an end fifty four years of electric tramcar operation in Sunderland. The route was lined with people, many of whom returned to the Wheatsheaf where some souvenir collecting took place!

The headmistress of Bede Girls Grammar School launched an amazing attack on horror comics at the school's junior speech day. She said that it should be an offence to supply horror comics and to pass on the "wicked rubbish" contained within them. She said that she regarded it as good news to read that American horror comics would not be imported in Britain and she encouraged the town's parents to assist their children in cultivating the art of good reading.

In the climax to the long running illuminations saga, the Seaside Development Committee recommended that the town's seaside light show be suspended for three years. Expenditure for the 1954 season had exceeded budget while receipts were well below the estimated forecasts. Attendances at the illuminations had been gradually declining since 1950 and some of the Progressives on the town council were in favour of switching off the lights for five years. This letter proposal was defeated as was the motion to sell off the set pieces rather than hire them to interested parties.

Following the success of Sunderland Corporation's PAYE one man operated bus service between Hill View and Town, a second service was launched between Southwick and Grangetown.

1954

Right
Sunderland's biggest fire in post war years occurred on 14th December 1954 when Joplings' department store in High Street West was completely destroyed.

The four storey department store of Joplings was destroyed in Sunderland's biggest fire of the century on 14th December. The blaze raged for over three hours and, at its height, the glow of the fire could be seen twenty miles away as flames leapt several hundred feet into the air. One hundred firemen and twenty fire engines attended the incident. Eighty residents from the William Street area were evacuated from their homes under police supervision as their furniture was moved into nearby Charles Street. Damage was estimated at over £1 million but thankfully no one was injured. Later, Mr. Swan of owners Hedley & Swan addressed the store's workers at a meeting at the Havelock Cinema saying, "the building has gone but the spirit of Joplings has not gone. We shall be meeting the local Planning Committee to discuss building a larger new store." The news was greeted with cries of "For he's a jolly good fellow."

Right
A classic town centre scene from the fifties. A Sunderland Corporation tram clanks past the central railway station in High Street West

The Sunderland Echo
(82nd YEAR) and Shipping Gazette
County Final

1955

No. 26,079   WEDNESDAY, June 1, 1955.   THREE HALFPENCE

RAIL STRIKE: EDEN SUMMONS CABINET

Mrs Woods Storms At

Mr Baty

MRS Geraldine Woods, a 60-year-old widow, of Cholmondeley Gardens, London, to-day stormed into the lobby of the A.S.L.E.F. head-quarters in London and demanded: "Where is Mr Baty? I'll wring his neck."

She told embarrassed officials: "Because of the strike I've got to walk all the way up this hill. It's a pity Hitler isn't here. He would shoot a few of you."

Waving a bundle of newspapers under the officials' noses, she added: "If I had my way I'd drag you through the streets by the hair. It would do you good."

HAMMERS ON DOOR

Ignoring the protests of officials who hurried into the high lobby of the Edwardian mansion, she hammered on the oak-panelled door of the room in which Mr Baty was working.

"Are you him?" she demanded as the door opened slightly. Quickly the door was slammed.

As Mrs Woods stamped down the stone steps of the head-quarters she turned, waved her papers at the perplexed caretaker and shouted: "I'll bring back a deputation and make Mr Baty see me."

TRIUMPHANT RETURN

THE Tunisian Nationalist leader, Habib Bourguiba, returned in triumph to Tunis to-day after three years of French-imposed exile.

Thousands of Tunisians had gathered to greet the man who is regarded in Tunisia as the architect of the agreement with France which give internal autonomy to the protectorate.

Along the crowds massed on the Tunis quayside was an official reception committee, including Prince Chadly, son of the Bey, members of the Tunisian Government, and leaders of the Neo-Destour Party, of which Mr Bourguiba is chairman.

THE EDEN BRIDE.— Albert Spedding, of Henry, and Miss Margaret Ruell, of Ile Eden, who were wed in Castle Eden Church yesterday.

Union Chief Absent from T.U.C. Meeting

WHILE Britain struggled to get to factory, office, and shop on the second working day of the rail strike, the T.U.C. General Council to-day went into session at Transport House, London, to hear a special report on the emergency.

But Mr Jim Baty, General Secretary of the 70,000-strong Associated Society of Locomotive Engineers and Firemen, did not attend.

Meanwhile it was announced that the first Cabinet meeting since the Government was confirmed in office at the general election will be held at No. 10 Downing Street, to-morrow afternoon.

The Cabinet will have a full scale discussion on the strike situation. They will probably consider the final text of the Queen's Speech opening Parliament, which will now be delivered next Thursday instead of on the following Tuesday.

Sir Anthony Eden, who is at Chequers, was to-day in constant telephonic communication with Sir Walter Monckton, Minister of Labour, and other Ministers directly engaged in handling the crisis.

Stayed At H.Q.

It had been hoped that the presence of Mr Baty and Mr Jim Campbell, General Secretary of the National Union of Railwaymen, at to-day's T.U.C. Council meeting might prepare grounds for a meeting between the two unions. Mr Baty, however, remained at his union's H.Q. in London, where a spokesman said: "Owing to pressure of work, he is unable to go to the T.U.C. meeting."

Mr Campbell asked if there were any developments in the strike, replied: "There is no move in any direction at the moment, but we shall, of course, be having a report from the General Purposes Committee.

This report was prepared at yesterday's three-hour meeting of the T.U.C. General Purposes Committee. It was expected that after the General Council had decided on any steps to be taken, the problem would be handed back to this more compact committee.

General indications throughout the country to-day were that, despite the lack of trains, the trek to work and more smoothly than yesterday. Traffic control systems were streamlined after yesterday's experience and queues in many cities, including London, were not so long.

Many people set out to work earlier and in some areas—Birmingham, Bristol, Liverpool and the West Riding of Yorks—conditions were much easier, or, sometimes, almost back to normal.

WORKERS ADVISED TO USE TRAINS

SUNDERLAND Stationmaster, Mr G. C. Renton, said to-day that local trains are running half empty, and appealed for travellers on short - distance journeys to use trains rather than buses.

Mr Renton said that during the rail strike workmen's services on routes such as Sunderland to Newcastle and South Shields are being given priority.

"Despite this, most workpeople are queuing for buses and arriving at work or home late, when they could have walked straight on to a train" he said.

PITS WORKING

Durham Division of the National Coal Board is stockpiling at some of the collieries, but there is no hold-up of production. A statement issued by Mr Walter Rich, Public Relations Officer, this afternoon, said: "Yesterday's output of coal from Durham Division totalled 93,000 tons, which is a normal output for the first day after Whit.

"Movement by road, rail and sea, of coal and coke from collieries and coke ovens is up to expectations and to-day pits and coke ovens are all working."

He said that some stockpiling of coal is being carried out wherever necessary but so far it has been less than the N.C.B. expected. Everything indicates that coal and coke movements and coal stocking will continue on similar lines, but the situation should be more clear by mid-day to-morrow, Mr Rich said.

PIT HOLIDAYS

Next week-end the colliery holiday season begins at some collieries including Blackhall and the men are hoping that the situation will not worsen before they leave on Saturday for the fortnight's annual break.

Coal shipments to Seaham Harbour are little short of normal as Dawdon, Murton, South Hetton and Seaham collieries have direct access by colliery lines to the docks. The only colliery affected by the strike is Vane Tempest. One coal train is running from this colliery to the docks, making three trips a day, carrying about 800 tons of coal a day. A number of lorries, loading under a temporary conveyor, are running a shuttle service to the docks with about 300 tons a day. The balance of coal from Vane Tempest is being moved by road to I.C.I. at Billingham, the Northern Gas Board at Sunderland, and Hendon Paper Mills.

TRAIN TIMETABLE—See P5

For breaking a chair and four glasses in a Sunderland public house, Edward Evans, of Dene Terrace, Charlton's Buildings, Ferryhill, was fined a total of £2 with 10s costs. He pleaded guilty to wilful damage, and to being drunk and disorderly in Moor Street.

HELD UP by the rail strike are these trucks loaded with scrap iron at Sunderland docks.

SWISS POLICE SWOOP ON COMMUNISTS

SWISS Federal Police announced that at dawn to-day they had carried out a large-scale roundup of Italian Communist Party members in ten Swiss towns.

A communique said there were indications that the Italians had been making an organized attempt to form cells to extend their grip over the Italian colony in Switzerland, and to operate a political information service.

The communique said: "Certain Antonal police authorities recently received information concerning the activities of Communists of Italian nationality in Switzerland.

"Investigations established that these foreign subjects, inscribed members of the Italian Communist Party had grouped themselves in our country to carry on organized activity, aimed particularly at forming cells in their places of work.

"They also tried by devious manœuvres to extend a direct grip over the Italian colony in Switzerland."

The towns where police raids took place were Zurich, Winterthur, Frauenfeld, Shaffhausen, Baden, Gebenstrof, Brugg, Zofingen, Basle and Binningen.

PIPE-LINED COAL

COAL is to be pumped 108 miles through a pipeline across Ohio from mines near Pittsburgh, U.S., to a Cleveland electric power station.

The coal will be broken into small pieces at the Pittsburgh mines and then fed with water into the pipeline. Pumping stations will push it along and at the other end the water will be drained off and the coal stored.

The pipeline, to be started soon, is expected to cost more than £2,856,000.

Terrorists Killed

Ten people were killed and ten injured in the past 24 hours in renewed outbreaks of terrorism in the French North African territories of Morocco and Algeria.

Docks Dispute "Can Be Quickly Settled"

THE National Dock Labour Board stated this afternoon that the total number of dockers on strike to-day was 19,795—about 40 less than yesterday. There were 156 ships idle, 79 undermanned and 115 fully manned. A spokesman said that the position was much the same as yesterday.

Mr W. Newman, Acting General Secretary of the Stevedores' Union, said to-day: "This strike could be settled immediately if the employers would put a full stop a few words earlier.

"They have said they are quite prepared to negotiate with us if the Transport and General Workers' Union agrees. If they will knock off the words after the strike.

"It is as simple as that. With-with us' we are ready to settle be settled at once.

Mr Newman said he expected need never have started and can out those few words, this strike an answer to-morrow from the T.U.C. General Council meeting to-day to the striking union's Mr Newman said he expected an answer to-morrow from the

T.U.C. General Council meeting to-day, to the striking union's question about 10,000 stevedores in Northern ports who were allegedly poached from the Transport and General Workers' Union by the National Amalgamated Stevedores' and Dockers' Union.

The stevedores' union is asking what happens to these men if a disputes tribunal decides they should be returned to the T. and G.W. Union and if the men refuse to rejoin.

The Jamaica Banana Board to-day reversed its decision to suspend banana shipments to Britain after hearing the British dock strike was not preventing the discharge of bananas in London.

**INDUSTRIAL ACTION BROUGHT
RAIL CHAOS TO BRITAIN IN 1955.**

In 1955 ...

Parliament voted to keep the death penalty.

Birds Eye fish fingers first went on sale.

Disneyland opened in California.

The BBC first demonstrated colour television.

Dixon Of Dock Green was first shown on BBC Television.

The U.K.'s first Wimpy Bar opened.

Commercial Television started in London.

Non-stick pans first went on sale.

Long running television programme This Is Your Life was first screened.

Ruth Ellis became the last woman to be hanged in Britain.

Diesel trains began to replace steam locomotives.

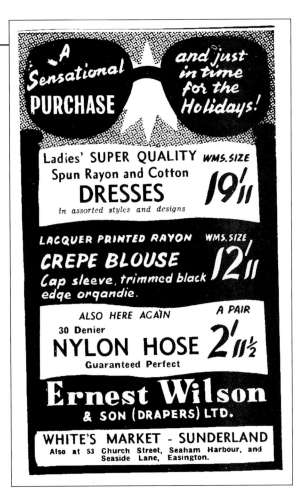

Left
A popular fifties brew.

Right
Ernest Wilson's fifties merchandise on sale at White's Market.

In Sunderland in 1955...

Sunderland Corporation Highways & Planning Committee approved plans submitted by the Northern General Transport Company to build the town's first permanent bus station on a site between Stockton Road and Park Lane at a cost of £100,000.

It was alleged that residents on the town's new Hylton Castle housing estate were being exploited by operators of travelling shops. The operators were said to be touring Hylton Castle and other estates on the edge of the town's boundaries and were selling groceries at prices greatly above those charged at town centre shops. A Hylton Castle councillor claimed that a typical family of two adults and two children were having to pay £1 per week more when shopping by this latest method. The chairman of the General Purposes Committee suggested that the matter should be referred to the Chamber Of Trade for investigation.

When the Hylton ferryboat filled up with water at rising tides, it overturned and sank. A 12 foot cable which was capable of transporting six passengers was brought into service to replace the 30 foot long, flat bottomed ferryboat which had been used to move forty passengers at a time. However, the cable kept springing a leak and at that point it was necessary for passengers to stand on their seats during the river crossing. The local ferryman was employed to bale out the cable during crossings although one passenger commented that he considered it to be unsafe while another said that he had noticed large blocks of ice over nine inches thick floating down the river and rocking the boat which made travelling unsafe.

Above
One of half a dozen trading kiosks which were opened at Seaburn in 1955 and which were popular with tourists throughout the late fifties and early sixties.

Hedley & Swan, owners of Joplings store which had been destroyed by fire in December 1954, announced that it hoped to build a new store on the old High Street West site. The company later said that the new store would be built at the junction of John Street and St. Thomas Street. An official of the company commented, "The site finally chosen is more centrally situated and, being larger than the High Street West site, it provides ample space for future development. The new store must be larger than the old one to meet the demands of a rapidly expanding business."

When the shipyard of Joseph L. Thompson & Sons took only 22 weeks to build a 18,000 ton motor tanker from keel to launching stage, it was congratulated on a "remarkable feat" by a director of the ship's owners. The remarkable delivery time of *The Sheaf Holme* compared with one of thirteen months for its sister ship *The Sheaf Royal* and was attributed to a large-scale reorganisation of Thompson's yard.

Left
State of the art fairground attractions at Seaburn in May 1955.

A 26 year old mother of five appeared before Sunderland Magistrates accused of hitting her four year old daughter over the head with a poker and fracturing her skull. She assaulted the child after discovering that she had let an Electricity Board man into the house to cut off supplies. The woman, who lived in Hope Street, pleaded guilty to causing grevious bodily harm when she told magistrates that she had visited her sister to borrow some money to buy coal but, after being unable to borrow the cash, she snapped when told about her daughter's actions. "I knew my husband would hit me as I'd showed him up in front of the neighbours by having no lights in the house," she said.

A former Sunderland ice cream manufacturer Alexandro Fella told Sunderland Bankruptcy Court that when major suppliers re-entered the market after ice cream was de-controlled in 1950, his annual turnover fell from £63,000 to £9,000. Mr. Fella established his ice cream business on Wearside in 1938 from premises in Sorley Street and in 1947 he bought St.Paul's school in Hendon Road for £2,500 and converted the building into a factory.

A proposal to close grocery shops on Mondays was rejected by the National Secretary of the Grocers Federation who said that the proposal was impractical. He added, "It would find little favour with our customers whose convenience is the prime consideration. The suggestion to close all day Monday would leave thousands of housewives stranded for replenishment of food supplies after the weekend, particularly in view of the small proportion of housewives with a refrigerator."

Sunderland's rural medical officer said that working class housewives tended to put on weight during their thirties by denying themselves the more expensive and protective foods which they instead gave to their husbands. They ate starchy food themselves such as bread and dripping or bread and jam and got fatter as they got older with some working class women reaching eighteen stone in weight. His comments were made following a medical survey of 238 women in the Tunstall and Silksworth areas.

Left
Not a single construction seen on this fifties photograph at Wheatsheaf corner has survived to this day.

Right
Roker baths Road in 1955 in the days when a mineral railway line ran across the road.

Sunderland's confectioners protested against the sale of twopenny packets of chewing gum which contained pictures of nude or scantily clad girls in the form of playing cards. The products were imported from Denmark and had been sold elsewhere in Britain since 1954 but caused an uproar upon their arrival in Sunderland. The secretary of the Sunderland Branch of the Confectioners Association said, "I think it is a very low type of business which uses indecency to boost sales. I have seen some of the cards and they are disgraceful. The ace of hearts shows a nude woman and the nine of diamonds depicts a girl wearing a very, very small brassiere and just a tiny piece of cloth around her middle." One Sunderland confectioner with a shop situated near to a school refused to stock the chewing gum and was disgusted that children regularly visited his shop asking for the confectionery as "the cards inside are good."

Trouble floated into Sunderland's seafront when two hundred tons of seaweed covered large areas of beach at the Cat & Dog Stairs at Roker. In places, the seaweed was up to three feet deep and there was concern that it would swell after it had dried out. The cause of the problem was identified as eddies which had been set up by the presence of a sewer pipe which acted as a breakwater. The floating seaweed was swept in by whirlpools on both sides of the pipe and then left behind as the tide receded. One course of action to overcome the problem was the removal of the weed to Fulwell tip where it could be stored for subsequent use as a fertiliser. However, it was then discovered that if the weed was piled at certain points on the beach, the currents caught it and carried it away. Sunderland's entertainments manager Mr. William Holden said, "Once it has swirled away, the old seaweed never comes back again. It is always a new lot."

Right
Demolition work in progress
at Strawberry Farm Cottage
in January 1955.
The 150 year old building
stood at the bottom of
Strawberry Bank and at
one time functioned as a
public house.

Left
The Barracks in 1955.

The Sunderland branch of the National Hairdressers Federation announced that the cost of men's haircuts would increase by 3d. The increase meant that the cost of a short back and sides would cost 2s in the town centre and 1s 9d on the outskirts of town. Although the national body recommended a minimum charge of 2s 6d, Sunderland exercised its local autonomy and decided upon an amendment vote on the lower charges. The prices were enforced in all NHF Salons.

The Ministry of Housing & Local Government was asked by Sunderland Corporation to approve a 30 acre extension to Barnes Park which would take in the valley from Springwell Road to an area west of Ettrick Grove. Barnes Park was opened in 1909 and at 40 acres was the biggest park in Sunderland.

Sunderland Corporation told its council house tenants that they could no longer expect a free load of good garden soil to go with their new council houses. If families found that plants would not grow in the gardens of their new houses, it was their responsibility to do something about it. A free supply of good quality soil had been introduced to tenants of new houses in December 1953 but the Estates Committee accepted a recommendation to discontinue the service in June 1956 as it was not financially viable.

The *Sunderland Echo* reported on the sad story of Cedric the River Wear swan which was found dead floating in the river near to Short Brothers shipyard. Cedric's tale of woe began when he was discovered with a broken leg by shipyard workers. The PDSA were called but Cedric struggled from the river bank and into the water, scorning medical aid from the PDSA boat as he nestled behind other swans in the river near Alexandra Bridge. His bobbing motions in the water earned him the nickname Bobalong.

Sunderland sent its two MPs back to Parliament at the General Election. Mr. Paul Williams (Conservative) was returned with a majority of 1,774 for Sunderland South and Mr. Fred Willey (Socialist) was returned with a majority of 2,836 for Sunderland North. Despite an increase of over 3,000 in the number of electors in Sunderland, there were fewer votes cast than at the 1950 or 1951 General Elections. The turn out of 76.57% meant that 93,318 people went to the poll compared with 98,302 in 1951 and 100,702 in 1950.

At its June meeting, the Estates Committee approved the erection of an unprecedented 127 television aerials on council houses.

Sunderland slipped back into fourth position in Britain's shipbuilding league for the period from April to June. In doing so, it exchanged positions with third placed Belfast. The River Wear's total output for the quarter stood at 202,760 tons compared with Belfast's 223,690 ton.

As a result of the dock strike, many of the town's housewives ran short of Danish butter and bacon. Some grocers refused to sell supplies to other than regular customers although one shopkeeper commented "We are fortunate because at this time of year (July), there is little demand for bacon." Meanwhile, the Sunderland Grocers Association made strong protests to the principal tea companies that their profit margins were inadequate on tea which retailed at 1s per quarter. One grocer commented that the members should ask the companies point blank to give grocers a better ratio of profit while some members suggested that the products should be withdrawn from the shelves. The latter idea was defeated when it was pointed out that there was a big demand for cheap tea in working class areas and traders were therefore obliged to stock it.

Plans for Sunderland's biggest ever private housing estate were approved by the Highways Committee. A 57 acre site to be known as Dene Lane Estate was designated as the development area with local company Lane Fox & Co. being the principal building contractors.

Above
Less traffic congestion than today in Hylton Road. The former police station is in the foreground.

The Sunderland Echo

and Shipping Gazette

(83rd YEAR)

No. 26,288   WEDNESDAY, February 1, 1956.   THREE HALFPENCE

ROADS FREEZE-UP IS WORST SINCE '47

Coldest Night for Nine Years

TRAFFIC dislocation was worse today than at any time since the great freeze-up of 1947, said the Automobile Association. Practically every county in England and Wales was in the clutch of ice and snow.

"Driving conditions are as bad as we can remember," said an A.A. spokesman. The situation was worst in the industrial Midlands where hundreds of miles of roads were frozen into what could almost be described as an icefield. Every road in the Birmingham - Coventry - Lichfield area was completely icebound.

Altogether the freeze - up covered roads in an area of more than 50,000 square miles. Roads in Scotland and West Wales were not seriously affected.

Last night was the coldest for nine years and on the Air Ministry roof in London the thermometer dropped to 21 degrees. At noon it was still only 23 degrees, compared with 30 yesterday.

One of the lowest temperatures recorded was at Elmdon, near Birmingham, where it was 10 degrees—22 degrees of frost. London suburban rail services were delayed up to an hour, mainly through frozen points and signals. Long-distance trains arriving in London were also delayed, and some services were cancelled.

An Eastern Region spokesman said that as soon as the anti-freeze salts had liquified the ice on points they were frozen again by the icy wind.

"Frightening"

Severe frost during the night caused the races at Hurst Park today to be postponed until tomorrow and Thursday's programme, with the exception of the Tudor Rose Hurdle, abandoned.

Traffic on roads in almost every county from Lands End to John o' Groats was reduced to a dangerous slithering crawl, said the Royal Automobile Club at midday.

In the extreme northern counties of England, where it was again snowing heavily, patrols described conditions on some roads as "frightening."

The Great North Road between Newcastle and Berwick and the Newcastle-Carlisle roads were passable only with extreme care, and the main Newcastle-Durham road was not advised for light traffic.

OVERHEARD

TWO engineers talked to each other on the telephone today—and through a fault in a cable their conversation was broadcast to the nation on the B.B.C.'s Light Programme.

A B.B.C. spokesman told a reporter: "It happened some where between 11 a.m. and noon. It was fairly intelligible—between two engineers, either ours or the G.P.O.'s I don't know."

The conversation was heard all over the country on the Light Programme. It caused by a line fault between Belfast and Glasgow on a Post Office cable."

For the Old Folk

...ton - on - Trent Voluntary Association announced that in view of the recent spell of cold weather it [...] spend £250 by making an immediate distribution of free groceries and coal to poor and old people of the town.

SUPPORTERS.—A few of the 3,500 York supporters gone to Sunderland by train today to cheer their side in the fourth-round F.A. Cup replay at Roker Park. See Page 7.

SEAMAN DREW KNIFE ON COMMODORE: FIVE-YEAR SENTENCE

AN ABLE SEAMAN who drew a clasp knife and stabbed twice at the Commodore of Chatham Naval Barracks was sentenced to five years' [impris]onment and "to suffer the consequential [penaltie]s involved" at a Chatham court-martial.

Seaman Jack Cook (19), [was] guilty to lifting up a [knife] against Commodore Coleridge.

[Cir]cumstantial letter outlining [the] prosecution's case said [that on] January 19 at about [noon] Cook was standing in [front of] a high desk near the [door] to a room on the first [floor of the] Commodore's offices. [Commod]ore Coleridge was [sitting] three feet away on the [other sid]e of the desk, writing, [in] his jumper, said the [letter.]

Petty Officer R. Anderson pulled Cook away by the neck, and grasped his right wrist, while Petty Officer G. Tinn seized the knife and threw it to the deck.

PREVIOUS OFFENCES

Lieut. J. Utting also closed with Cook and brought him under control.

Several previous naval offences were proved against Cook, including a conviction for desertion in November 1955. Last month he deserted again.

For this second offence he appeared before the Commodore on January 27, and was sentenced to 90 days' imprisonment and dismissed the Service.

The defending officer, Lieut. Commander R. H. C. Ellis, said that since leaving his boys' training ship Cook had been unable to settle down, and for two years had been to get his discharge by one means or another.

Ship Stoned

[MILIT]ARY school students [who] stoned a British [cam]p and overturned it in a Cyprus village today, [according] to reports reaching [us.] The reports said that [the stude]nts, who were behind [their] positions, dispersed [when] soldiers in the jeep [fired shots] over their heads.

ARRESTED

[The Russi]an naval ships patrol-[ling the] North Sea arrested a [...] Soviet fishing vessel [...] night for "fishing [in] Norwegian territorial [waters.] The drifter was [towed] to the West coast port [...] and to join 12 other [...] drifters and the 7,000-[ton deplo]t ship Tambov, [...] for the same reason [Monday] and Tuesday.

Plan to Close North End of Town Station

A PLAN to close the war - scarred North End of Sunderland Central Station met with the full approval of the Corporation General Purposes Committee last night.

Alderman Joseph Hoy, Chairman, told the Committee that the British Railways authorities want to demolish the North End and replace it with a departmental store. An arcade of shops would also be built to link Union and Station Streets.

It is evident that the south entrance to the station in its present form could not cope with the additional passengers who could use it if the North End were closed.

British Railways has prepared a scheme which, at a cost of a quarter of a million pounds, would double the South End accommodation, providing additional booking offices, waiting - rooms and other facilities.

A new road would be built immediately to the east of the Athenæum Street entrance leading into what is now the car park at the rear of the Town Hall. Vehicles using this route would cross by a new road into Union Street, a proposal which would require the enclosure of part of the station. A section of the station would still remain open to allow smoke from locomotives to escape. The replacement of steam trains by diesels on the coastal line will, however, lead to the elimination of this smoke.

British Railways and Sunderland Corporation have been discussing these proposals and the only difference of opinion is over the position of the store in relation to High Street West.

STORE SET BACK

The railway authorities have suggested that the store should extend over the present taxi stand but the Corporation wants the building to be set back so that a small square can be laid out.

The Committee decided last night that the store should be set back 30 ft from High Street West. A cantilever method of construction would enable the floors above ground level to cover a bigger area.

The alterations to British Railways proposals will now go

Continued in page 7

N.C.B. CHAIRMAN DIES AT 66

Was to Have Retired in July

SIR HUBERT HOULDSWORTH, Chairman of the National Coal Board since 1951, died suddenly at his home in Lincoln's Inn, London, today. He was 66.

Sir Hubert was at his office at the Board's Victoria Headquarters as usual yesterday, and appeared to be in good health.

His five-year term of office as Chairman of the Board was to expire on July 31 this year.

SIR HUBERT

and it was announced two weeks ago today that he would be succeeded then by Mr. James Bowman, the vice-chairman.

Sir Hubert was created a knight in 1944 and received a baronetcy in the New Year Honours. His baronetcy was gazetted only last night.

Sir Hubert was the second chairman of the Coal Board, succeeding Lord Hyndley. Before that he was chairman of the Board's East Midland Division for five years.

In his earlier years he was a lawyer. He became a K.C. in 1937.

His cheerfulness and ready smile won him popularity both with his own officials and those of the National Union of Mine-

Continued in page 7

OUT OF ACTION

DERWENTHAUGH coking plant, near Blaydon, may be out of action for 24 hours as a result of an accident there today. The Tyneside Division of the Northern Gas Board has issued an urgent warning to all consumers to economise as much as possible. Tomorrow, industry may be seriously affected. A coke discharging car in the coking plant was derailed and overturned.

Queen and Duke Fly to Northern Nigeria

THE QUEEN and the Duke of Edinburgh today left the Nigerian capital by plane for the high plateau of the Moslem Northern Region, which covers two thirds of the vast colony.

They left exactly on time at 9.58 a.m. in the Royal plane for the 352-mile journey to Kaduna, which takes them over jungles and mangrove swamps.

ARAB LAND

The Queen and Duke again drove through cheering crowds in Lagos this morning on the 14-mile drive to Ikeja Airport, where the Royal plane was waiting to take the party on the second part of their tour of Nigeria.

For the next six days the Queen and Duke will live in a different world—an Arabic land of minarets, arid semi-desert, open parkland and grass savannahs, gradually merging into the sands of the Sahara.

The Royal couple are to spend three days at Kaduna. Tomorrow the Queen will hold there the first durbar of her reign and the first by any British monarch since the famous Delhi durbar held by her grandfather, King George V, in India 44 years ago.

In Kaduna, which is situated more than 2,000 feet above sea level on a tributary of the River Niger, the Queen and Duke will also attend a State banquet, garden party and investiture, see a parade of schoolchildren, visit the Regional Legislature and watch traditional dancing.

IN 1956, THE DECISION WAS TAKEN TO DEMOLISH THE NORTH END OF SUNDERLAND'S CENTRAL RAILWAY STATION AND TO REPLACE IT WITH A DEPARTMENT STORE. AS THE *SUNDERLAND ECHO* REPORTED AT THE TIME, THE ORIGINAL INTENTION WAS TO BUILD AN ARCADE OF SHOPS TO LINK UNION STREET AND STATION STREET.

In 1956 ...

The Eurovision Song Contest was shown on television for the first time.

The Royal Mint produced the last farthing coin.

Love Me Tender became Elvis Presley's first film release.

It cost 2¹/2d to post a letter and 4s 10d to buy a gallon of petrol.

Cartoon character Andy Capp made his first appearance.

A pint of beer cost 1s 9d.

Top athletes Tessa Sanderson and Sebastian Coe were born.

Jim Laker took nineteen wickets for ninety runs against Australia at Old Trafford.

Prince Rainier of Monaco married Grace Kelly.

8% of houses in the UK owned a refrigerator.

The first British nuclear power station was opened at Calder Hall.

The Clean Air Act was introduced when coal fumes were outlawed in London.

Below
Sofsil apparently doubled the bubbles!

Right
Sunderland's
own packet tea
in the fifties.

In Sunderland in 1956...

Sunderland Corporation reaffirmed its determination not to give any financial assistance to Newcastle Corporation in its efforts to develop Woolsington as a regional airport. The chairman of Sunderland's General Purpose Committee which made the decision said, "The government recommends that municipalities throughout the country should be encouraged to develop their own aerodromes. The principal objections of north east local authorities to finance the Woolsington scheme is that Newcastle Corporation would continue to exercise control over the development and running of the aerodrome, once the improvements have been made." He added that it was unlikely that Sunderland would develop its own municipal airport in the near future as this would be beyond the financial resources of Sunderland Corporation.

The big freeze of February dominated the *Sunderland Echo* headlines. When two main water pipes burst, water supplies in some areas of the town were thrown into chaos. A burst distribution pipe in Church Street, Deptford meant that residents' water supplies were completely cut off. Meanwhile, a combination of ground movement and frost resulted in the burst of an eighteen inch thick pipe in Newcastle Road. The *Sunderland Echo* reported that water from the burst pipe flowed down Mill Bank like a small river. Residents in Fulwell suffered low water pressure. The freezing weather also had an adverse effect on the mining industry as most collieries found it necessary to stockpile coal in pit yards as it arrived at the surface. The coal began freezing up in trucks as it arrived at loading points with the result that the shipment trucks were operating on a turn-around time of one third of normal. Bad weather also held up vessels in north east ports with the consequence that coal shipments were further disrupted.

The Cox Green ferry service closed on 12th February with the late evening crossing at 11.20pm. Villagers were subsequently faced with a five mile walk to Washington for shopping and the nearest post office and chemist. The 61 year old owner of the Barmston to Cox Green ferry had earlier announced his intention to discontinue the river crossing service, which had been run by his family for generations, by posting notices on both banks of the river. He told the *Sunderland Echo*, "In view of the adverse comments made about the operation of the Barmston to Cox Green ferry, I feel that the only solution is to relinquish all rights to it." For many years locals had campaigned for a footbridge to replace the ferry which they found to be unsatisfactory due to waiting time between crossings. It was operated on a part time basis and generated minimal income for the owner from the 1½d fare. The ferry was used extensively by the workforce of Washington Chemical Works where the owner himself worked.

Left
The South Hylton ferry, crossing the River Wear just prior to the cessation of the service on 12th February 1956.

Left
Sea coal gathering was a common
sight in more austere times.
This photograph was taken in 1956.

Right
A deserted Cox Green station in 1956.

In February, a massive blaze wrecked the House Of Grantham furniture store in Holmeside. The alarm was raised by members of the public at 9.30pm and such was the ferocity of the blaze that sixty firemen were still at the scene over four hours later. The *Sunderland Echo* reported flames leaping sixty feet from the roof of the store and at one stage the fire threatened to engulf adjoining properties as fears rose that the three floors of blazing furniture would get out of control. The incident occurred on a cold winter night and, incredibly, water actually froze on firemen's uniforms and icicles formed on the 100ft. turntable ladder. Some firemen were still at the scene of the charred building the next morning as people made their way to work.

Mr. Norman Morton, 45 year old manager of Sunderland Corporation Transport Department began an eight hour shift as driver of a double decker bus and said, "I am doing this to gain first hand experience of both conditions on the road and on the job. This week I am taking a full turn of duty on the backshift from Hylton Road Depot. Later, I'll take an early shift from Fulwell Depot on a bus serving the north side of the river." Few passengers identified him as the Transport Department manager although several people wondered about the driver in lounge suit and coat. Some bus crews suspected that his presence was to check on timetable schedules. One conductor commented, "At first we all thought it was a joke. It will do us a lot of good when he sees what we have to put up with."

Above
The central reading rooms and junior library facilities were accommodated in Fawcett Street during the fifties.

One of the town's major sources of employment, the furniture manufacturing industry, hit upon hard times as one third of the one thousand workforce began a short working week. The shortage of orders were not due to the credit squeeze of the time but to the prolonged spell of icy weather which had gripped the town and cut the wages of the shipyard men who were unable to work in the cold conditions. The resultant drop in spending power meant that several of the fifteen furniture manufacturing and upholstery firms in Sunderland witnessed rapidly diminishing order books. One Hendon company began working only on alternate weeks while a town centre based firm began a four day working week. A company spokesman commented, "This is the second successive year in which the furniture industry has been hit and naturally a lot of men are leaving the trade and finding work elsewhere. We are no longer attracting boys to the trade. Years ago, we had boys clamouring for jobs long before the end of term but so far not one has asked to come into the trade this year."

When a fire damaged the bar and music room of the Globe Hotel in High Street East, it lead to the discovery of a staircase which nobody knew about. The staircase was uncovered when firemen knocked down a wall in the hotel's music room to reach the seat of the fire (which had been smouldering for days!) and discovered that it lead to rooms which had once been used as living quarters. The fire had started beneath the fireplace in the music room and gradually smouldered along wooden beams under the floor.

A policeman was very helpful to a man who wanted to get away from his wife for the Easter holidays - he locked him up! The 51 year old man from Annie Street threw a bottle of beer into the centre of the road in High Street West and when approached by the policeman he said, "Lock me up. Owt to get away from the wife." He was found guilty of being drunk and disorderly and was fined £1.

The *Sunderland Echo* reported that tempers were hot in Sunderland's 'Little Egypt' where housewives in Canon Cockin Street and Hastings Street were up in arms over the Corporation Watch Committee's proposals to close their streets to traffic and turn them into playgrounds. The women organised a petition against the scheme and one organiser told the newspaper, "We are nearly all owner-occupiers and our rates have been increased by 50% under the revaluation. This scheme will turn our homes - worth over £1,000 - into slums. If the streets are closed with concrete posts, every one will have to use the back doors for weddings and funerals. We keep our own children off the streets so why should be have our street turned into a playground for other people's children." The Watch Committee eventually dropped the proposals to transform the streets - together with nine others in congested areas of the town - into play areas. The chairman of the Watch Committee said, "I can assure everyone that proposals of this nature will not be forced upon people against the great weight of public opinion. If the committee makes a decision which is popular, it gets credit for it. If it takes an unpopular course, it has to take the odium of it."

Above
Sunderland's infamous barrow boys doing a roaring trade on the bombed site of the former Empress Hotel in Union Street.

It was announced that Sunderland's ferry services, which were reputed to be the cheapest in the country, would be curtailed due to heavy financial losses. The Corporation Highways Committee were faced with the possibility of having to replace one of the two steam ferries but instead recommended a series of service alterations. One recommendation was that on each Saturday when their was no First Division game at Roker Park, a rowing boat should be used instead of the ferry after 2.00pm. Similar recommendations were made for each Sunday. At that time, 800 people used the ferry each day at a cost of 1/2d per journey. The passengers were mainly shipyard and ropery workers. Two ferries operated daily and these were the Sir Walter Raine (which had been commissioned in 1939) and the W.F. Vint which had plied its trade across the river for over a quarter of a century. The 1/2d toll was the same as it has been one hundred years earlier although the numbers of passengers carried had drastically reduced since 1936 with slum clearance in the East End and the closure of the old market.

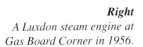

Right
A Luxdon steam engine at Gas Board Corner in 1956.

Eight men began work on sinking a shaft measuring 2,000 feet at Wearmouth Colliery. The work was part of a major reconstruction scheme which was aimed at increasing output as workings reached a greater distance into the sea bed. As well as improving the efficiency of the pit, the sinking of the shaft also ensured an adequate system of ventilation. At that time, Wearmouth Colliery workings reached about three miles out to sea. Work on sinking the first ever shaft at the colliery began in 1826 and at that time it was the deepest undersea mine in the world.

Sweet production began in the former St. Pauls School when a Sunderland manufacturer converted the premises into a factory to produce 20-25 tons of toffee and chocolate. The factory served as an extension to the company's premises in Lombard Street, Hendon which had been established for twenty five years.

When a man was suspected of consuming alcohol outside of licensing hours, a policeman stood on the shoulders of his colleague and looked through a four inch gap at the top of the window of a bar at the Prince Of Wales public house. From his vantage point, the policeman reported that he witnessed the man drinking from a pint glass. The time was 11.03pm and the man was arrested for drinking after hours. He was fined £3 and the licensee was fined £5 for supplying the drink.

1957

Sunderland Echo

& Shipping Gazette
LUNCH EDITION
No. 26,693 (84th YEAR) WEDNESDAY, MAY 22, 1957. TWOPENCE.

ROKER CLUB MANAGER IS FINED £200

Secretary Is Exonerated: Five Players Get Benefits Deferred

THE joint commission of the Football Association and Football League, which has been inquiring into the affairs of Sunderland A.F.C., today followed up its severe penalties on directors of the club — announced on April 10—by fining Mr Bill Murray, the club manager, £200 and imposing forfeits upon five players.

Ray Daniel, Billy Elliott, and Ken Chisholm (now with Workington) forfeit two years' qualification for benefit or accrued share of benefit and Willie Fraser and Johnny Hannigan forfeit six months. Club secretary, Mr George Crow, has been informed that his explanation to the commission is accepted and that no action will be taken against him.

Daniel and Elliott were due to benefits next year and Fraser and Hannigan in 1959 and 1960, respectively. Still to be dealt with are allegations that illegal Cup bonuses were paid to other members of the club. This will be the subject of a further meeting.

Trevor Ford, who wrote stating that he was unable to obtain leave of absence to attend the Commission's meeting in Sheffield on Friday, will be asked whether he elects to attend a further meeting of the Commission or be dealt with in his absence in accordance with the provisions of F.A. rule 45 (e).

Full Scope

Thus the full scope of punishments inflicted upon the club and its members as a result of the disclosure that the sum of £5,427 14s 2d had been accumulated through illegal transactions is that directors Mr E. W. Ditchburn (Chairman) and Mr W. S. Martin have been suspended for life; Mr S. Ritson and Mr L. W. Evans suspended sine die; Col. J. Turnbull, Mr S. S. Collings, Mr J. Reed, and Mr J. Parker severely censured; a £5,000 fine on the club; Manager Bill Murray fined £200, and five players forfeiting between them a total of £1,050.

Since the total of wages forfeited by the players during the 22-day period of their sine die suspensions after they had refused to answer questions put to them by the Commission in Manchester on April 25 is roughly £270, the total monetary imposition upon the club and its members is £6,520.

Statement

A statement issued by the Commission today reads: "At a meeting of the Commission held in Manchester on April 25 the following players were suspended sine die from April 26 for refusing to answer questions asked by the Commission, K. Chisholm, R. Daniel, W. H. Elliott, W. Fraser, J. Hannigan. A decision with regard to Trevor Ford was deferred.

The Commission held a further meeting at Sheffield on May 17 when the following attended: Mr J. H. Pigg, accountant to the club; manager Mr W. Murray; secretary Mr G. Crow; and players K. Chisholm, R. Daniel, W. H. Elliott, W. Fraser, J Hannigan, and G. Aitken.

"The players were represented by Mr J. Hill (Chairman) and Mr C. Lloyd (Secretary) of the Players' Union.

"The Commission heard evidence from all the above-named persons. The players admitted that they had received illegal payments from the Sunderland F.C. but not the amounts specified in the charges.

Decisions

"The Commission decided that:

(1) The sine die suspension imposed on the players at the meeting of April 25 be lifted from May 17;

(2) K. Chisholm, R. Daniel, and W. H. Elliott shall forfeit two years' qualification for benefit or accrued share of benefit;

(3) W. Fraser and J. Hannigan shall forfeit six months' qualification for benefit or accrued share of benefit;

(4) W. Murray (manager) be fined £200;

(5) The explanation of G. Crow (secretary) be accepted and that no action be taken against him;

(6) Inquiries with regard to alleged illegal payments of cup bonuses to other players of the Sunderland F.C. be dealt with at a future meeting;

(7) The out-of-pocket expenses of the players who attended the meetings on April 25 and May 17 be refunded to them.

"Player T. Ford attended the meeting on April 25 and denied the charges made against him. He wrote stating that he was unable to obtain leave of absence to attend the meeting on May 17. The Commission decided to defer a decision in his case in order that he may elect whether to attend before the Commission again or to be dealt with in his absence within the provisions of F.A. Rule 45 (E)."

The Commission added notes to its statement explaining that in arriving at its decisions on the five players it had taken into account the suspensions imposed on April 25 and that in the case of Mr Murray it took into account "the fact that Murray acted under instructions."

The five players at first refused to speak before the Commission, on union instructions following legal advice. Last week they changed their minds "in view of altered circumstances" as Chisholm put it after the Sheffield meeting.

Told of the punishments on the players, Mr Jimmy Hill, the union chairman, said: "I have no comment to make. The question will have to go before the union committee to find out their opinion and whether we propose to take any action in the matter."

Campaign

He added that the union was still collecting signatures of players willing to "confess" to having received under-the-counter payments, in their campaign for a general inquiry into soccer finance.

"Conditions for collecting them are difficult, however, with the players on their summer break," said Mr Hill.

In its original findings the Commission declared that Mr Murray was "an active participant in these irregularities, and the secretary, Mr Crow, had knowledge of them."

It then added: "Due consideration should be given to the fact that, as servants of the club, they were in the position of either having to carry out their instructions or face the consequences of their refusal to do so."

THE WORK OF THE INQUIRY

THE joint commission, which was appointed by the F.A. Joint Advisory Council in January, consists of Mr Arthur Drewry (Chairman), Sir Leslie Bowker (vice-chairman), and Mr F. Barrett, representing the F.A., and Mr Arthur H. Oakley (President, now retired), Mr J. Richards (vice-president), and Mr H. Shentall (vice-president), of the Football League, has held six meetings so far.

The pattern of its investigations has been:

SHEFFIELD (March 7): A preliminary meeting attended by Mr E. W. Ditchburn, Mr W. S. Martin, Mr W. Murray, and Mr G. Crow.

YORK (March 29): The entire Sunderland board, together with Mr Murray, Mr Crow, club accountant Mr J. H. Pigg and Mr R. H. C. ...ron, a Newcastle solicitor, were called.

LANCASTER GATE (April 6): Meeting in private, the Commission made decisions on the evidence obtained at York and four days later announced suspension of half the Sunderland board, severe measures upon the remainder, and deferred decisions in the cases of Mr Murray and Mr Crow.

MANCHESTER (April 25): Called to this meeting were Mr Murray and players Billy Elliott, Ray Daniel, Willie Fraser, Johnny Hannigan (all Sunderland), Ken Chisholm (Workington), and Trevor Ford (P.S. Eindhoven). Also present were Mr Jim Hill (Chairman) and Mr Cliff Lloyd (Secretary), of the Players' Union. No action was taken in the case of Ford, but the remainder of the players were suspended sine die for refusing to answer questions put to them.

LANCASTER GATE (May 8): The shortest meeting on record, at which the only decision taken in the absence of Sir Leslie Bowker and Mr Drewry was to fix the date of the next meeting.

SHEFFIELD (May 17): Messrs Murray, Crow, and Pigg, together with all the suspended players, were interviewed. Also before the Commission was Sunderland player George Aitken, who answered questions on the allegations that illegal cup bonuses had been paid to players. The Players' Union were again represented by Messrs Hill and Lloyd.

MID-DAY COURSE SELECTIONS

YORK: 2.0, Impala; 2.30, ...; 3.0, Jaunty Scot (n.b.); ... French Beige (nap); 4.0, ...de; 4.30, Cock of the ...

SALISBURY: 2.0, Ben Arthur; ... Master Nicky; 3.0, Joyeux ...; ...30, Misbehave; 4.0, Verve; ... Vicunia.

FINED £200

MR BILL MURRAY, Club Manager.

Exonerated

MR GEORGE CROW, Club Secretary.

Bill Dodgin To Manage Italian Club

Bill Dodgin, former Fulham and Brentford manager, has agreed to join the Italian First Division soccer club, Sampdoria of Genoa, as manager next season, the club president, Signor Alberto Ravano, said in Genoa last night.

He said that Dodgin was in the director's box at Genoa last Sunday and watched Sampdoria beat Naples 1—0.

"After the match Mr Dodgin agreed to take the job of manager next season. Nothing has been signed yet," Signor Ravano added.

Sampdoria, who are fifth in their league championship, bought centre forward Eddie Firmani from Charlton Athletic for £35,000 two years ago.

EGYPT THROWS OUT THE CROWN

It has been decided that the crown and all other Royal insignia should be removed from the Egyptian Parliament building where the National Assembly will be holding its meetings in the future

The main chamber of the Assembly will feature a large painting illustrating the various stages of the Egyptian people's struggle up to the revolution of 1952.

Rise In Japanese Illegal Drugs

Stimulating drugs, considered to be as dangerous as narcotics, are being produced and marketed in increasing amounts in Japan, despite efforts by police and doctors to wipe out the traffic.

A police spokesman said that there were 5,106 cases of illegal production of drugs in Japan during 1956. He said there was a growing tendency among drug dealers to organize themselves into gangs, many of whom employed juveniles as pedlars.

Late Course Wire

YORK

3.30—HORNBEAM.

WHY TAIL-ENDERS ARE GETTING RUNS

FREDDIE Trueman, batting number nine 63; Brian Statham, also number nine 53; Tony Lock, number eight 32 not out. Our bowlers, and England men at that, have made some good scores this week.

But it would be stretching the imagination to call any of them all-rounders, although Lock plays strictly along the line of the ball for much of the time.

Trueman and Statham are more in the category of hit or miss. The fact that they have scored these runs is not really surprising.

Pitches recently have been on the sticky side, with the bowlers holding the upper hand. Recognized batsmen without real class, have struggled by orthodox methods. Under such conditions, the tail enders, to whom batting averages mean little, hold a better chance of a reasonable return by less approved tactics.

The present averages show the advantage of ball over bat, despite the limitation of leg side fieldsmen. With little over a week to go to the end of May, many of the country's leading run-getters in normal times are finding great difficulty getting near 500 runs, let alone the 1,000.

That target was last reached before June by Sir Donald Bradman and Bill Edrich in 1938.

On the other hand, Tony Lock is nearly half-way towards 100 wickets. He has taken 44 at just over seven runs apiece. Statham and Trueman have each taken 36 wickets.

Drivers Are Warned About Big Meals

The German Medical Information Service has warned motorists to avoid driving immediately after a heavy meal. When the stomach is digesting a full meal, the brain gets less blood. Consequently the driver feels tired and is less attentive, the Service said. That increases the danger of accidents.

It advised motorists on long journeys to take a hot meal during the drive, if possible, but to have a stroll before getting back behind the wheel.

SCANDAL AT SUNDERLAND AFC AS THE FOOTBALL LEAGUE AND THE FOOTBALL ASSOCIATION INVESTIGATED ALLEGED FINANCIAL IRREGULARITIES WITHIN THE CLUB.

In 1957 ...

The Hula-Hoop became Britain's best selling toy.

Top television shows the Army Game and Emergency Ward Ten were first shown on ITV.

Harold Macmillan replaced Anthony Eden as Prime Minister.

TV detector vans first took to the roads.

Britain's first H Bomb was exploded.

The cost of a television licence rose from £3 to £4.

BBC Television show Tonight became the country's first news magazine programme.

Premium Bonds first went on sale.

The European Common Market was formed.

The first frisbees went on sale.

Left
Palmers from the days when it was a major trading name in Sunderland.

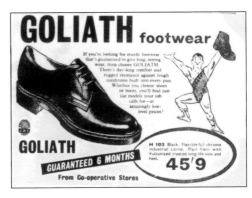

Above
The good old CWS was sited in Green Street and sold shoes which were guaranteed for six months.

In Sunderland in 1957...

Left

Johnny Bollands was Sunderland's first choice goalkeeper during the1956/1957 football season. He signed for Sunderland from Oldham Athletic for a fee of £2,500.

A 31 year old ship, the 5000 ton Cairnesk, was finally withdrawn from service amidst comments from its owners that it had "completed a record of remarkable service which must be unique for a cargo ship engaged in regular liner service." The vessel had been operated by the Cairn Line exclusively in the Canadian trade during its 31 years of service and had covered a total of 207 double Atlantic crossings involving 1,250,000 miles of steaming in that time. The owners said that the ship had been a credit to the skill of the shipyard men of Sunderland who had built her during the darkest days of the 1926 depression. The Cairnesk had been built by William Pickersgill & Sons in the middle of the post war slump of the twenties at a time when yard after yard was closing on the Wear. Pickersgill's shipyard was one of the few yards with their gates still open at that time and during the year of the Cairnesk's construction, only six other ships were built on the Wear.

Sunderland's municipal piggeries, which had provided seven million rashers of bacon for the North East breakfast tables since 1941, closed following a Cleansing Committee recommendation to the town council. Chairman of the committee said that the piggeries and associated waste food plant had not cost the ratepayers a penny to run during their sixteen year existence but added that the wartime conditions which led to their establishment no longer applied. He thanked the town's housewives for the wonderful help and cooperation which they had given since 1941 during which time eight thousand householders had put out swill each week for collection by the cleansing department. He also thanked cafe and hotel owners as well as factory canteens for their support. The piggeries were situated at Fulwell and the waste food plant at Deptford.

Sunderland became one of the first local authorities in the country to establish a technical school for girls when the Minister Of Education approved the town's plan to run West Park School as a girls only facility. Under the scheme, no boys were admitted to the school from 1957 onwards with a 'girls only' intake of ninety pupils in each of the following five years. This important development in education served to thrust Sunderland to the forefront of visionary local education authorities. At that time, very few other towns had considered the necessity to provide girls with technical training during normal school life.

Above
The disruption caused by tram track removal during the mid to late fifties can be seen from this photograph taken at Gladstone Street in 1957.

Two streets of 86 year old colliery houses at Tunstall, New Silksworth were described at a public enquiry as being "totally unfit for habitation by present day standards." It was claimed that the only effective course of action would be to demolish the houses in Tempest Street and Vane Street as they were old and worn out with a complete lack of facilities. In summing up, the public enquiry concluded that "the houses are long passed their useful life. Nothing can be done with them now."

Engineers at the Southwick & Sunderland south docks started work on building a giant factory plant which would convert sea water into drinking water at a rate of one million gallons per day. The completed plant was eventually exported to Ecuador to help overcome the country's shortage of drinking water.

The Highways & Planning Committee recommended the acceptance of proposals to convert the first floor and gallery of the former YMCA building in Fawcett Street into a dance hall with a capacity to accommodate two hundred people. Under the proposals, the hall would be used for Saturday night dances and as a dance studio during the remainder of the week.

Austin & Pickersgill announced reconstruction plans for their Southwick shipyard which would enable them to build ships up to 23,000 tons capacity. At that time, such a capacity was double the size of any previously launched vessels. Once the construction was completed, it was claimed that the shipyard would be the most modern yard of its size anywhere in the world. The managing director of the company said, "If we are to keep pace with the the competition already upon us and to complete the changeover from rivetting to welding, it is essential that we should modernise our facilities."

Three days after the publication of the Medical Research Council's report on the relationship between smoking and lung cancer, The *Sunderland Echo* reported that the 25 a day man on Wearside was still smoking as many cigarettes as ever. The town's tobacconists reported business as usual with no decrease in sales. "The cancer scare has not affected us one little bit," said the manager of one major distributor in Sunderland. Meanwhile, the Northern General Transport Company had not yet discussed the possibility of banning smoking on the lower decks of its double deck buses to bring them in line with corporation buses.

Residents in Chester Road were terrorised by gangs vandalising derelict properties in the nearby Johnson Street area of the town. After bulldozers left for the night after demolishing houses in Johnson Street, gangs descended upon the area to vandalise the delapidated buildings and to remove whatever they could lay their hands on. One housewife told a *Sunderland Echo* reporter, "A house has only to be vacant for a few hours before the hooligans take over. Windows are smashed, doors carried away, cupboards set alight, pipes wrenched out and even the brickwork torn away." Chester Road residents said that their lives were being made a misery as gangs from all parts of the town descended upon Elgin Street and Albert Street. They lit fires and made themselves at home while others were seen to carry away parts of staircases and fireplaces. They came prepared for their hauls with horse and carts and even trucks. A nearby resident told the *Sunderland Echo*, "It's time the council did something about it. At the very least they should give us police protection."

Sunderland witnessed its biggest holiday exodus to date as 30,000 shipyard and engineering workers began their annual holidays. Travel agents reported a 25% increase in demand for continental holidays with the most popular destination being Jersey, followed by Spain and Italy.

Objections were raised by High Barnes residents to proposals to build a public house in Wavendon Crescent on the grounds that it would lower the standard of the neighbourhood and create a great deal of noise which would, in turn, result in a depreciation in house values. The objections were overruled by the Ministry Of Housing & Local Government after Sunderland's Licensing Planning Committee expressed the view that the local amenities should be upgraded for the area's estimated population of 3,000. The plans included the provision for a public house as there were only two others within a half mile radius.

Left
Generations of sunbathers have walked down the Cat and Dog Stairs to the beach at Roker.

Right
The cars are the main giveaway to the age of this view of Gill Bridge Avenue. The photograph was taken in 1957.

The impromptu choir which began singing on a late night "dancers special" bus were using words which were not quite proper for mixed company, according to a police constable who was on board the bus at the time. When the policeman left his seat and asked the singing quartet to reduce its volume and to moderate the language of the lyrics, one of the singers replied, "If you are a cop, come into the cafe and I'll buy you an ice cream but wear your helmet. In the meantime, keep your mouth shut." When summoned for making excessive noise and singing to the annoyance of other passengers, the four pleaded guilty to the first charge but not guilty to using obscene language. When confronted with a typed sheet containing the offending words, they all shook their heads emphatically while one man added, "That wasn't our song. We used some of these words but that wasn't the song." Each of the four men were fined £1 on each of the two charges.

Sunderland Juvenile Court was told that an £11 a week miner was living with his wife and five children in a kitchen and small scullery which was used as a bedroom. Two of the miner's sons were appearing in court accused of attempted housebreaking and theft. The Chairman of the court said, "This is one of the worst examples of overcrowding which has come to our notice in years." The defending probation officer told the court that the two brothers were living in such overcrowded conditions that they preferred to be out of the house and that this had led to their involvement with crime.

Above
*Pedestrians cross Fawcett Street near the former
Gaumont Cinema.*

Right
A rare close up of Mackies Corner clock.

Sunderland's ferry service finally closed on 18th July when the W.F Vint made its last river crossing dressed with coloured flags and with civic dignitaries crowded on to the deck. The Chairman of Sunderland's Highway Committee described the occasion as "a sad farewell to an old tradition." As the boat pulled into the Monkwearmouth landing for the last time amidst cheers from the large crowd of sightseers, he said, "I regret to have to perform this ceremony tonight but it is inevitable. There is just not the need for the ferry as in the past. It is losing £6,000 of ratepayers' money each year.

A double deck Corporation bus made the trip around Sunderland's south docks to see whether the roads were suitable for passenger carrying vehicles. The River Wear Commission were of the opinion that the roads were too narrow to carry buses and had never been laid out for such use. The investigation was carried out following long standing complaints from two thousand shipyard, engineering and port workers that there was no adequate bus service to take them to and from work. It was eventually agreed to provide a service to run from the South Docks via Barracks Street bank to the corporation Quay and back into High Street East by the gate at Pottery Buildings. The bus service meant that workmen no longer had to make the long walk up Barracks Street bank to the Corporation buses which, in turn, were often delayed while waiting for the last man to arrive at the top of the bank.

KNIGHTALLS
for Everything Furnishing
SIMPLE OUT OF INCOME PURCHASING SERVICE
2, 3, 4 OLDSTORD STREET

Sunderland Echo and Shipping Gazette
Football Echo EDITION
No. 26,981 (85th YEAR) SATURDAY, APRIL 26, 1958. TWOPENCE

SALES SERVICE SPARES
for
LAMBRETTA
Vespa, DKR Dove, Zundapp Bella, Diana
at your
OFFICIAL DISTRIBUTORS
COWIES
Vine Place (opp. Tech. Coll.) Sunderland 58045
Millfield Sunderland 70691

SUNDERLAND GO DOWN

How the Teams Fared Today

DIVISION I

ningham 0 Leicester C. 1 (Half-time: 0—0)
nley ..... 3 Bolton W. . 1 (Half-time: 2—0)
lsea ..... 2 Man. U. .... 1 (Half-time: 2—1)
n. City .. 1 Aston V. ... 2 (Half-time: 1—2)
vcastle . 1 Leeds U. ... 2 (Half-time: 0—1)
ts F. .... 0 Everton ..... 3 (Half-time: 0—0)
tsmouth 0 Sunderland 2 (Half-time: 0—1)
ston NE 3 Arsenal ..... 0 (Half-time: 2—0)
ffield W. 2 Wolves ..... 1 (Half-time: 2—0)
tenham . 2 Blackpool .. 1 (Half-time: 2—0)
st Brom. 4 Luton Town 2 (Half-time: 1—2)

	P.	W.	D.	L.	F.	A.	P.
erhampton	42	28	8	6	103	47	64
on N.E.	42	26	7	9	100	51	59
nham	42	21	9	12	93	77	51
Brom	42	18	14	10	92	70	50
hester C.	42	22	5	15	104	100	49
ey	41	20	5	16	77	73	45
pool	42	19	6	17	80	67	44
Town	42	19	6	17	69	63	44
Utd.	42	16	11	15	85	75	43
ea	42	15	12	15	83	79	42
Forest	41	16	9	16	68	62	41
nal	42	16	7	19	73	85	39
ngham	42	14	11	17	76	89	39
Villa	41	16	6	19	72	65	38
n W.	42	14	10	18	65	87	38
ton	42	13	11	18	65	75	37
U.	42	14	9	19	51	63	37
ster C.	42	14	5	23	91	112	33
astle U.	41	12	8	21	72	78	32
mouth	42	12	8	22	73	88	32
erland	42	10	12	20	54	97	32
eld W.	42	12	7	23	69	92	31

DIVISION II

Bristol City 1 Swansea .... 2 (Half-time: 1—1)
Cardiff City 3 Fulham ..... 0 (Half-time: 2—0)
Charlton A. 3 Blackburn . 4 (Half-time: 1—3)
Doncaster . 1 Ipswich ..... 1 (Half-time: 1—1)
Grimsby T. 3 Bristol R. .. 2 (Half-time: 2—1)
Huddersf'ld 0 Lincoln City 1 (Half-time: 0—1)
Leyton O. .. 0 Sheffield U. 1 (Half-time: 0—1)
Liverpool ... 1 Barnsley ... 1 (Half-time: 1—1)
Middlesbro' 1 West Ham . 3 (Half-time: 1—3)
Rotherham 1 Notts Co. .. 3 (Half-time: 1—0)
Stoke City . 2 Derby Co. .. 1 (Half-time: 2—0)

	P.	W.	D.	L.	F.	A.	P.
West Ham Utd.	42	23	11	8	101	54	57
Blackburn R.	42	22	12	8	93	57	56
Charlton A.	42	24	7	11	107	69	55
Liverpool	42	22	10	10	79	54	54
Sheffield Utd.	41	21	9	11	74	49	51
Fulham	40	19	11	10	93	57	49
Middlesbrough	**42**	**19**	**7**	**16**	**83**	**73**	**45**
Ipswich T	42	16	12	14	68	69	44
Huddersfield	42	14	16	12	63	66	44
Stoke City	42	18	6	18	75	73	42
Bristol R.	42	17	8	17	85	80	42
Leyton O.	42	18	5	19	77	79	41
Grimsby T.	42	17	6	19	86	83	40
Barnsley	42	14	12	16	70	74	40
Cardiff City	41	14	9	18	62	74	37
Derby County	42	14	8	20	60	81	36
Bristol City	42	13	9	20	63	88	35
Rotherham	41	14	5	22	64	98	33
Swansea Town	42	11	9	22	72	99	31
Notts County	42	12	6	24	44	80	30
Lincoln C.	41	10	9	22	52	81	29
Doncaster Rov.	42	8	11	23	56	88	27

DIVISION III (N)

Barrow ..... 0 Halifax ..... 3 (Half-time: 0—2)
Bradford ... 3 Workington 3 (Half-time: 0—1)
Bury .... 2 Crewe A. .. 0 (Half-time: 0—0)
Carlisle U. . 0 Bradford C. 3 (Half-time: 0—2)
Chesterfield 2 Darlington . 0 (Half-time: 1—0)
Hartlepools 2 Mansfield .. 0 (Half-time: 2—0)
Oldham A. 0 Rochdale .. 0 (Half-time: 0—0)
Scunthorpe 2 Chester ..... 1 (Half-time: 1—1)
Southport .. 1 Hull City ... 2 (Half-time: 1—1)
Tranmere .. 2 Gateshead . 1 (Half-time: 1—1)
Wrexham .. 1 Accrington 0 (Half-time: 0—0)
York City .. 0 Stockport .. 0 (Half-time: 0—0)

	P.	W.	D.	L.	F.	A.	P.
Scunthorpe	44	27	8	9	83	48	62
Accrington	45	25	10	9	83	56	60
Bury	46	23	10	13	94	62	56
Bradford C.	45	21	14	10	73	49	56
Hull City	46	19	15	12	78	67	53
Mansfield T.	45	21	8	16	97	92	50
Chesterfield	45	18	14	13	71	69	50
Halifax T.	45	19	11	15	79	68	49
Stockport Co.	46	18	11	17	74	67	47
Rochdale	45	19	8	18	78	63	46
Wrexham	45	16	13	16	60	61	45
Gateshead	**45**	**15**	**15**	**15**	**68**	**73**	**45**
Oldham A.	45	14	17	14	71	81	45
Tranmere R.	45	17	10	18	80	75	44
Hartlepools Utd.	**45**	**16**	**12**	**17**	**72**	**74**	**44**
Carlisle U.	**45**	**19**	**6**	**20**	**79**	**75**	**44**
York City	**44**	**15**	**12**	**17**	**62**	**76**	**42**
Workington	45	14	13	18	72	78	41
Barrow	46	13	15	18	66	74	41
Darlington	**44**	**16**	**7**	**21**	**75**	**85**	**39**
Bradford	46	13	11	22	68	95	37
Chester	45	12	13	20	68	80	37
Southport	46	11	6	29	52	88	28
Crewe Alex.	46	8	7	31	47	93	23

DIVISION III (S)

Bournem'th 1 Swindon T. 1 (Half-time: 0—0)
Brentford .. 4 Port Vale .. 1 (Half-time: 2—1)
Colchester . 1 Plymouth .. 2 (Half-time: 1—0)
Coventry C. 1 Gillingham . 1 (Half-time: 1—1)
Crystal Pal. 1 S'thampton 4 (Half-time: 0—3)
N'thampton 1 Southend U. 3 (Half-time: 1—1)
Norwich C. . 1 Aldershot .. 3 (Half-time: 1—1)
Shrewsbury v. Exeter C. (Half-time: 0—0)
Torquay U. 2 Newport Co. 2 (Half-time: 1—2)
Walsall ..... 4 Millwall .... 2 (Half-time: 3—2)
Watford .... 0 Brighton ... 1 (Half-time: 0—0)

	P.	W.	D.	L.	F.	A.	P.
Plymouth A.	46	25	8	13	67	48	58
Brighton	44	23	12	9	82	63	58
Swindon T.	46	21	15	10	79	50	57
Brentford	45	23	10	12	81	56	56
Reading	46	21	13	12	79	51	55
Southampton	45	22	10	13	110	68	54
Norwich City	46	19	15	12	75	70	53
Southend Utd.	44	20	11	13	82	53	51
Bournemouth	45	20	9	16	78	73	49
Newport Co.	46	17	14	15	73	67	48
Queen's P.R.	45	17	14	14	61	65	48
Colchester U.	45	16	13	16	73	77	45
Northampton	45	19	6	20	84	73	44
Crystal Palace	46	15	13	18	70	72	43
Watford	45	13	16	16	59	71	42
Port Vale	45	16	10	19	66	55	42
Aldershot	46	12	16	18	59	89	40
Coventry	45	13	13	19	59	78	39
*Shrewsbury	44	14	10	20	48	68	38
Walsall	46	14	9	23	61	75	37
Torquay U.	45	11	12	22	47	72	34
Gillingham	45	12	9	24	49	79	33
*Exeter City	45	11	9	25	57	98	31
Millwall	46	11	9	26	63	91	31

* Late kickoff

Amateur International

England ... 1 France .... 1 (Half-time: 1—1)

Your Pools Check

LITTLEWOODS

: 111 X22 22X 2X2 1X (28)
: 11X 222 2X2 X21

VERNONS

: 112 222 2X2 21X 21 (26)
: 12X 222 2X2 221

SHERMANS

: 11X 222 2X2 2X2 1 (26)
: 11X 222 X22 X21

ZETTERS

: 111 X22 X22 21X (23)

EMPIRE

Pts: 112 X22 X2X 212 (24)
Res: 112 22X X21 X2

SOCCER

Pts: 1X2 2X2 X2X 21X (27)
Res: 1X2 2X2 X2X 211

HOMES

ENH'SEMUIR	BURY
ANGERS	TOTTENHAM H
WDENBEATH	WEST BROM A.
STIRLING	ST JOHNSTONE
YDE	CARDIFF C.
ONTROSE	BRENTFORD
ARTLEPOOLS	SCUNTHORPE
HEFFIELD W	CHESTERFIELD
RESTON N.E.	WREXHAM
ALSALL	STOKE CITY
HELSEA	GRIMSBY T.
URNLEY	TRANMERE R.

AWAYS

OUTHEND U.	ALDERSHOT
INCOLN C	BRIGHTON
STON VILLA	SUNDERLAND
WANSEA T.	AIRDRIE
LYMOUTH A.	DUNDEE UTD.
EST HAM U.	LEICESTER
ULL CITY	BLACKBURN R.
EEDS UTD.	BRADFORD C.
VERTON	HALIFAX T.
RBROATH	SOUTHAMPTON
OTTS CO.	SHEFFIELD U.

DRAWS

YORK CITY v STOCKPORT
OLDHAM v ROCHDALE
BRADFORD v WORKINGTON
BOURNEMOUTH v SWINDON
EEN OF SOUTH v ST MIRREN
MORTON v DUNFERMLINE
KILMARNOCK v RAITH ROV.
COVENTRY v GILLINGHAM
DONCASTER v IPSWICH T.
LIVERPOOL v BARNSLEY
TORQUAY v NEWPORT

ORTH-EASTERN LEAGUE

arl'gt'n R. 2 Spennymoor 1
ockton ... 2 Carlisle R. . 5
nd. R. ... 4 Horden 0
. Stanley 0 Consett 2

Highest Score

EAST STIRLINGSHIRE 5
RANGERS 5

Highest Aggregate

Charlton 3, Blackburn 4

Scottish Cup: Final

Clyde .... 1 Hibernian .. 0 (Half-time: 1—0)

Scottish League (A)

Dundee ..... 1 Airdrie ...... 3 (Half-time: 0—1)
Kilmarnock 1 Raith R. .... 1 (Half-time: 1—0)
Motherwell 1 Th'd L'nark 2 (Half-time: 0—0)
Queen of S. 2 St Mirren .. 2 (Half-time: 1—2)
Rangers .... 5 Aberdeen .. 0 (Half-time: 3—0)

UPS AND DOWNS

DIVISION I

Champions—Wolverhampton Wands.; runners-up, Preston N.E.
Relegated — Sheffield W. and Sunderland.

DIVISION II

Promoted — West Ham, Blackburn.
Relegated — Doncaster R.

LEAGUE III (NORTH)

Promoted — Scunthorpe U.

Victory at Pompey Was Too Little and Too Late!

LEICESTER ALSO WIN

Sunderland today lost their distinction of never having played in any but the First Division. In spite of a last-ditch victory, they are relegated for the first time in 68 years. Leicester City also won.

PORTSMOUTH - - 0 SUNDERLAND - - - 2

RAIN fell steadily an hour or two before the start of Sunderland's vital League game against Portsmouth at Fratton Park this afternoon. Because the ground was firm this morning, however, it meant that only the surface itself would be soft.

Portsmouth expected quite a big attendance but the rain must have kept many would-be spectators away. The covered accommodation was popular enough but there were huge gaps in the uncovered portions of the ground which meant that there were little more than 15,000 present at the start.

Sunderland turned out as selected but Portsmouth had to make a late change after Dougan had failed to pass a fitness test. The centre forward position was taken over by Crawford.

PORTSMOUTH
Uprichard
McGhee Gunter
Dickinson Rutter Carter
Harris Gordon Crawford Bernard Govan
O
Grainger O'Neill Kichenbrand Revie Fogarty
Pearce Hurley Anderson
Elliott Hedley
Fraser
SUNDERLAND

Referee: Mr R. J. Leafe, of Nottingham.

Revie won the toss and Sunderland took advantage of the cross-wind ... well-timed tackle by Elliott checked a Pompey move down the left and when Kichenbrand got back to lend a hand the ball was driven down the middle

By
ARGUS

where O'Neill tried unsuccessfully to move ahead of McGhee and Rutter. Anderson, Revie, and O'Neill combined well in mifideld but the wing half's pass down the wing was out of play before Fogarty could reach it.

Players of both sides were having difficulty in getting a foothold on the treacherous surface.

Revie was in trouble near the corner flag when challenged by Gunter. He managed to get the ball over at the second attempt but there was no Sunderland player near enough to make contact with him.

Two Chances

Grainger handled the ball in bringing it under control when moving inside and from the resulting free kick Portsmouth built up an attack which gave them two chances of going ahead. The first came when the ball was lobbed over Hurley's head and Crawford

Continued in Back Page

LATEST

4.30—RIPON
1. Golden Gittell (20-1); 2. Judicature (4-1. f); 3. Dollar Help (100-8).

4.45—WORCESTER
1. Paul Jones (11-10. f); 2. My Pick (2-1); 3. Smart Catch (3-1).

4.50 SANDOWN
1. Snow Cat (11-2); 2. Aliede (8-11. f); 3. Vomer (7-1).

5.0 RIPON
1. The Mongoose (4-1); 2. Lacydon (5-6. f); 3. Silver Town (100-8).

Derness SC 1. Belmont SC 3
Roker Meth RC 0. Hendon 0
John Laing & Co 1. Doxford App 4
Dock St Meth YC 0. Doxford App 0
Corinthians AFC 0. TLP Jun. 6
Lambton Manors 5. S... RC 2
Lambton Manors 4. Thomp. MH YC 3
Silksworth Mechs 5. Melton W St 0
Steels SC 2. S Shields Corin 3
Penrith 1. Crook 0
Sund Forge 4. Johnsons Wel 1
Shiney R St O... 3. Murton J 3
[illegible]
Pallion Marine [illegible] SC 3

SHOP AT Binns

Driway Week

Buy the ...

MONARCH WEATHERCOAT

THE FINEST RAGLAN MADE! All the finest traditions of English tailoring are combined to give you the exclusive DRIWAY Monarch Weathercoat—supreme in style, fit and quality.

£13/19/6 and £14/19/6

ALWAYS AT THE TOP OF HIS FORM!

Boys' raincoats of navy, fawn, or grey proofed gaberdine, with protective cape of proofed interlining across shoulders, front and back. Drop hems on coat and sleeves. 24in.-46in.

87/6 To 154/6

Always an Excellent range of Boys' Schoolwear.

BINNS MEN'S SHOP HOLMESIDE

BINNS LTD. SUNDERLAND Tel 4411

26TH APRIL 1958 WAS A BLACK DAY FOR SUNDERLAND AFC AS THE CLUB WERE RELEGATED FROM TOP FLIGHT FOOTBALL FOR THE FIRST TIME IN THEIR HISTORY.

In 1958 .....

The first Parking Meter was introduced in Britain.

The Hovercraft was invented.

The Munich Air Disaster claimed the lives of seven Manchester United football players.

The Queen performed the opening ceremony at Gatwick Airport.

Athlete Daley Thompson was born.

BBC Television sports programme Grandstand was first transmitted on 11th October.

The first CND protest march was staged.

Birth defects attributed to Thalidomide were first detected.

The Common Market was first set up, with Britain excluded.

Television programme Blue Peter was first screened.

The first tower blocks were built in Britain.

Above
Jerome's photographic shop which catered for the more descerning customer.

Right
In 1958 there was a Sunderland Building Society.

In Sunderland in 1958...

Diesel trains made their first appearance on the Sunderland - South Shields and Sunderland - Newcastle lines on 18th August. As a result, the majority of passenger trains which passed through Sunderland central station were diesel powered from that date onwards. The first diesel train to be seen in Sunderland was in October 1954 on a test run, twelve months before the introduction of regular diesel services on the Newcastle - Sunderland - West Hartlepool - Middlesbrough run.

Coal shipments from the Port Of Sunderland during the first six months of the year showed a huge drop of 144,607 tons compared with the corresponding period for 1957. One reason for the shortfall was the number of power stations which had made the switch from coal to oil burning. Other factors included British Railways' ongoing conversions to diesel train operation and the increasing use of hydro-electricity in overseas territories. As a consequence, there were many cases of coal stock-piling at local collieries.

Not only did Sunderland top the league of north east towns and cities for post war house building, it also set the pace for slum clearances. A total of 677 houses were demolished in the town between 1st January 1955 and 31st March 1958. Meanwhile, by 30th June 1958 over 13,000 post war houses had been built in Sunderland while a further 1,917 homes had been built by private contractors.

Above
A view of Austin's Quay in 1958 when Sunderland was a major shipbuilding centre.

Above
Tents, deck chairs and packed beach scenes such as this were commonplace at Seaburn throughout the fifties.

Wires between electric pylons at Gillbridge caused havoc among the town's racing pigeon fanciers. In an eighteen month period a total of 216 pigeons had been killed as a result of flying into the wires while countless other birds such as sparrows, crows and seagulls had also met their deaths in a similar fashion. Racing pigeon enthusiasts in the Gillbridge Avenue area protested about their losses and demanded that action be taken to remove the 'death wires'.

In July, the Sunderland Empire became one of six Moss theatres to be given a 'summer rest' by its owners. The theatre closed following a show with singing footballer Colin Grainger. The official reason given for the closure was said to be lack of available shows due to the decision of several stars to go into summer shows at holiday resorts. Despite an external re-decoration of the theatre during its enforced period of closure, there was a distinct lack of information about a re-opening date. While announcing the Empire's 'summer rest', the manager commented, "We are not getting the support of the public even for shows which do good business in other towns."

Many Wearsiders took advantage of the new personal loan service being offered by some banks. High on the list of reasons given for loan applications was expenditure on house decoration, furniture and cars. The most popular applications were for loans in the region of £100 to £200 while the maximum loan permitted was £500. The manager of one bank told the *Sunderland Echo*, "Many of our applications are from ordinary working class people who see this as an opportunity to get something they have wanted for a long time."

On 9th September a bulldozer knocked down the 200 year old walls of Strawberry Farmhouse which had recently become the target for vandals. At one time, afternoon teas of strawberries and cream were served in the gardens of the building.

Above Left
*Youngs, Bergs, Brechners and Louis were just some of
the traders in Crowtree Road when this photograph*

Above Right
*A well known fifties sight. The clock at Robson's
flour mill in Chester Road.*

Many Wearside miners were temporarily transferred to Boldon, Hylton and Westoe collieries while major re-construction work was carried out at Wearmouth. The purpose of the work was to develop undersea reserves of coal to the east of Wearmouth Colliery with the eventual aim of increasing production to one million tons. The work involved sinking a 24 foot diameter shaft to a depth of 2,100 feet while surface re-construction work included plans to build a new washery to replace the hand picking belts and dry cleaner. It was hoped that the electrification of the colliery could be completed by 1966 at which point manpower would rise by 600 to 2,400. Wearmouth would then become one of the most economical and productive collieries in the Durham coalfield.

Chimney fires in Sunderland were becoming so frequent and increasingly dangerous that the town's fire department made a special appeal to householders to do more sweeping on their own account. The Chief Fire Officer reported a big increase in chimney fires in his report to the Watch Committee. In a nine year period domestic fires had soared to a new all time record. In 1949, the fire department attended 130 chimney fires in Sunderland. The number increased to 301 in 1953 and to 402 in 1957. In a public statement, the fire department said that all householders should ensure that their chimneys were professionally swept three times per year and in addition they should remove loose soot from the lodges and chimney sides each time a fire was laid. The Chief Fire Officer commented, "It would save a lot of work if every morning the person laying the fire used a longer than average brush to sweep down all the loose soot which he or she can reach." A problem highlighted in the statement was the ever increasing shortage of chimney sweeps, particularly when spring cleaning time came around. The situation had been made worse by the gradual decline in numbers of chimney sweeps as fewer youths than ever were joining the trade.

Left
Sea Road in 1958 at a time when car ownership was much lower than it is today.

Sunderland's war against litterbugs warmed up when the town's Cleansing Committee authorised its inspectors to take the names and addresses of anyone seen dropping litter in the town. Employees of the Parks Department and Seaside Development Committee inspectors were given similar powers. Officials were instructed to approach offenders tactfully and to ask them to pick up their litter and place it into a bin. Only if they failed to get cooperation would the official put the new Litter Act into effect and record the offender's details. During the first month of the enforcement of the act nobody appeared before Sunderland Magistrates charged with a litter offence. Bus tickets were said to be the main items of discarded litter.

At a time when many bus operators in County Durham were experiencing a fall in the number of passengers carried, more people used Sunderland Corporation buses during the second quarter of the year than in any quarter during the previous eight years. During April - June, a total of 21,810,601 passengers were carried on the town's buses. The busiest route was the Circle, followed by Red House - Villette Road and Pennywell - Grangetown.

1958

Local brewers expressed concern about the number of workingmen's clubs which Sunderland Corporation were allowing to be built alongside the sites of public houses on the town's new council estates. Thriving clubs already existed at Pennywell and Thorney Close and others were planned for Farringdon, Hylton Castle and Hylton Red House estates. The Northumberland & Durham Brewers Association wrote to the corporation to point out that the proliferation of workingmen's clubs was not envisaged at the time of agreeing public house rentals and that they considered a retrospective adjustment to be appropriate.

Sunderland Town Council discussed the first stage in the layout of the town's proposed new housing estate at Town End Farm.

When a corporation rent collector called on a Hylton Castle housewife, he was asked to go to another house while she searched for her purse. When the rent collector returned, she was waiting behind the door with an axe which she used to strike him on the head. When the collector eventually managed to disarm the woman, he asked her to let him out of the house so he could go to the hospital to have his injuries treated. The housewife refused to unlock the door and said that she would treat the injuries herself from her ambulance box. The collector had to resort to breaking a window in the house to attract the attention of neighbours who came to his rescue. The woman who owed £6 9s in rent plus arrears was taken to hospital for a physical and mental examination.

Above
Crowds gathered in December 1958 to witness the launch of the Nordic Heron.

Sunderland Echo
& Shipping Gazette
SIX O'CLOCK

No. 27,205 (86th YEAR).   THURSDAY, JANUARY 15, 1959.   TWOPENCE.

Sunderland Gives The Macmillans Their Friendliest Reception On North-East Tour

CHEERS EVERYWHERE FOR THE PREMIER

Shopgirls Welcome Him As He Walks Down Fawcett Street

SUNDERLAND people today gave the Prime Minister, Mr Harold Macmillan, and Lady Dorothy Macmillan, their friendliest reception in their three-day tour of the North-East, which ends tonight. There were smiles, cheers, and handshakes everywhere they went.

People were very happy to welcome the Premier and his wife, and the visitors responded with good humour, a thought for everyone, including the maids who looked after them in their hotel, and a keen interest in everything they saw.

After seeing the big modernization scheme going ahead at the Sunderland shipyard of Joseph L. Thompson and Sons Ltd., and watching hundreds of men at work on the 34,500-ton Nordic Heron, at her fitting-out berth, the Premier said: "This has been one of the most impressive parts of the whole tour."

The Theme

That was the theme of their tour in Sunderland which began with a walk along Fawcett Street this morning. They each had a thought for activities great and small.

The entire staff of one grocer's shop got a big surprise when the Premier shook them all by the hand and congratulated them on announcing a reduction in the price of eggs.

The Prime Minister obviously endeared himself as a "man of the people" regardless of politics. There were cheers from shop girls, shipyard workers and women at factory gates, as well as from party supporters.

It was a tour which boosted Wearside — and pleased the Macmillans.

They looked fresh after a good night at their hotel. They breakfasted on corn flakes and two boiled eggs each and then Mr Macmillan read his mail—which was not heavy—made by special delivery.

Hatless and with a broad smile, Mr Macmillan, with Lady Dorothy, stepped from the Grand Hotel into a cheering crowd of people as the Town Hall clock struck ten this morning.

They smiled and waved to

Continued in Page 8

The Prime Minister seen shaking hands with women shoppers in Fawcett Street on his way to the Town Hall. —S.E.

MEETS YOUNGEST WORKER AT LOCAL SHIPYARD

THE youngest apprentice fitter working on the Nordic Heron at the Sunderland shipyard of Joseph L. Thompson and Sons Ltd., had the most exciting moment of his career when he was introduced to the Prime Minister today.

"Do you enjoy the work here," Mr Macmillan asked 17-year-old John Walmsley, of Ferndale Terrace, Pallion, who has worked at Thompson's shipyard for two years. John replied that he did and that it was a good start to his career to get the chance to work on the biggest ship to

be built on the Wear. The most frequent question asked during Mr Macmillan's visit to the North-East is: "Why doesn't he wear a hat?"

The answer was given today by Mr Anthony Barber, M.P. for Doncaster, who is the Prime Minister's Parliamentary Private Secretary.

"He never wears a hat," said Mr Barber. "It has been suggested several times that he should have some protection during this cold weather but he prefers to walk around bare-headed. He does have a hat—but it's in the car."

A NOISY—BUT SINCERE— GREETING AT THE ECHO

THE Prime Minister and Lady Dorothy were greeted with an ear-shattering "gerry"—caused by the banging of type on waste bins — when they entered the composing room of the Sunderland Echo today.

This is the compositor's own token of affection and is used on the occasion of an apprentice completing his time, and the departure or retirement of a colleague. Mr Macmillan smiled broadly and appeared to appreciate this novel greeting.

CHAIRMAN'S WELCOME

Earlier, on his arrival at the Echo offices, the Prime Minister was welcomed by Mr S. Storey, M.P., Chairman of Portsmouth and Sunderland Newspapers Ltd., Mr E. S. Hoare, General Manager (North); Mr T. G. Moore, General Manager (South); and Mr K. Lister, Assistant Editor (in the unavoidable absence of the Editor, Mr C. Cowley).

After meeting members of the editorial and commercial staff in the sub-editors' depart-

ment, Mr Macmillan moved into the library and Creed room, where they watched reports of national and international news coming in on the teleprinters. Lady Dorothy took

SOUVENIR

BEFORE he left Sunderland this afternoon for the Durham County School of Agriculture at Houghall, the Prime Minister received from the Sunderland Echo an album—bound in blue leather—of 18 photographs commemorating his visit to the town today.

a particular interest in the machine used for receiving photographs by wire.

Then the party moved into the composing room, where the Prime Minister's wife was presented with a posy of anemones, lily-of-the-valley, and fern by Miss Rita Whitfield, a 20-year-old copytaker.

Mr Macmillan chatted with Linotype operators and watched pages of the Echo being made up before going into the foundry and the Hoe printing machine-room, where

he met other members of the staff.

Afterwards, the party went into the Foster Press room, where Mr Macmillan started the presses which printed an early edition of the Echo to mark his visit to the town. Mr Macmillan and Lady Dorothy received their souvenir copies from Mr Storey.

Looking at the front page, which showed a photograph of him walking along Fawcett Street, only 45 minutes previously, the Prime Minister entered the Echo garage to be greeted by shoppers and workers gathered outside in Bridge Crescent.

Amid the cheers of the onlookers and Echo staff, Mr Macmillan and Lady Dorothy drove off to the North Sands yard of Joseph L. Thompson and Sons.

North Dish For Lunch

THE Prime Minister lunched in true North Country style at the Grand Hotel, Sunderland, today. Over roast beef and Yorkshire pudding he chatted with members of the Sunderland Conservative Association.

Later he left by car for Houghall, to tour the Durham County School of Agriculture and then on to a private meeting at the Conservative Hut, Birtley.

Hosts at the hut were women members of the Durham group of constituencies, with representatives from Chester-le-Street, Durham, Blaydon, and Easington. His tour ends in Newcastle tonight.

... This Was Unexpected

THE Prime Minister and Lady Dorothy received an additional welcome which came to them above the cheers of the crowd and the roar of the traffic as they left their town centre hotel this morning.

But the addition was accidental. A motor-car horn developed mechanical

trouble and refused to be silenced for several minutes as the driver frantically struggled under the bonnet to disconnect the wiring system.

With the help of a policeman, who was on duty outside the hotel, he eventually won his battle and drove off hurriedly, and slightly embarrassed.

Mr Macmillan chats with Mrs Margaret Dorward, forewoman cleaner at the Sunderland shipyard of Joseph L. Thompson and Sons Ltd., during his visit to the yard today. —S.E.

HAROLD MACMILLAN MET WEARSIDERS
ON A VISIT TO THE TOWN IN 1959.

In 1959 ...

The Russians produced the first photographs showing the far side of the moon.

The Hovercraft made its first commercial cross channel journey.

A refrigerator cost £63.

The Conservatives were re-elected at the General Election with a huge majority.

The first stretch of the M1 motorway was opened.

The Cod War began between British and Icelandic fishermen.

Margaret Thatcher entered parliament.

The first mini car was built.

Buddy Holly was killed in an air crash.

British television ownership soared to 9 million.

Television programme Juke Box Jury was screened for the first time.

Right
The latest goggle box, fifties style from Blacketts.

Left
Kennedy's had retail outlets at High Street West and Maritime Terrace; the latter of which was always curiously advertised as being at the top of Blandford Street.

In Sunderland in 1959...

The Ministry of Housing & Local Government rejected an application from Sunderland Corporation to build houses on an extension to its Grindon Village estate on land which was outside the borough boundary. The Corporation had applied for the compulsory purchase of 81½ acres of land and the application had been the subject of a public enquiry in September 1958. Objectors to the application were the two owners of the land; John T. Bell & Sons, Builders (of Newcastle) and C. Vaux & Sons (of Sunderland). The public enquiry decided that any building work should be undertaken by private companies and the houses offered for sale in the private sector. The development subsequently became the Hastings Hill estate.

The problems associated with starlings in the town centre was highlighted in the January edition of the *Sunderland Echo* when it was reported that more vigorous action was required to rid Sunderland of the birds. Councillor N. Waters told members of the town council, "All we are doing is trying to find a temporary solution instead of a permanent cure. We are not taking the matter seriously enough. The starlings were perched on the bridge so we put up those blinking lights and we drove them up the road to take command of Mackie's Corner. People passing by are in danger of being dive bombed and the filth on the bridge is unmentionable. Considerable sums are being spent on cleaning buildings in the town and they are being re-decorated by the starlings. We should get expert advice on this menace."

January saw extreme weather conditions hit Sunderland. Heavy snowfalls meant that even some main roads through the town centre were blocked for a short time. During the first half of the month it took over 18,000 man hours to keep the main roads and bus routes clear of snow and ice.

Left
The Savoy Cinema at Southwick in 1959. The bus on the left of the photograph shows its destination as Seaburn on route 18X. 'X' was used to signify a short working journey; route 18 terminating at Seaburn Camp at that time.

Left
Strothers, Swinhoes, car parking and two-way traffic in Blandford Street circa *1959.*

Right
A sleepy Silksworth scene from 1959.

The empty shell of the King's Theatre in Crowtree Road was living on borrowed time as plans were announced for its demolition. The building was hit by incendiary bombs and gutted during an air raid in May 1943. After the war, various trades were carried out in the basement of the building before plans were eventually unveiled for the construction of offices and shops on the site.

In April, strike action by seventy platers threatened to close three building berths at Austin & Pickersgill's Southwick shipyard. The company's managing director said that unless the platers resumed work and enabled the yard to function as normal, 452 men would be laid off leaving just 300 men to be employed with the fitting out of the 13,000 ton motor-ship Durham Trader. The platers' strike action surrounded the alleged wrongful dismissal of one of their number. The dispute was eventually settled and full production resumed.

'A little bit of courtesy goes a long way towards making life brighter.' Those were the sentiments expressed by the Northern General Transport bus company upon the launch of its so-called courtesy campaign. The campaign was aimed at passengers as well as at drivers and conductors and was said to acknowledge the inconveniences encountered in modern day travel with respect to traffic jams and hold-ups and to the strains which they imposed. The advice to drivers was to avoid jolts and jerks of the vehicles and to show special consideration to strangers whilst remembering to treat all passengers as human beings. Meanwhile, conductors were told to be courteous and polite even to 'awkward types' and to be sure that all seats were taken before showing passengers away. They were reminded that passengers were the object of the company's business and should not be treated as if they were an interruption to work. Finally, passengers were told to remember that courtesy was two way and they were asked to avoid tendering notes for a 1 1/2d ticket and to avoid the temptation of blaming the bus crews for delays to the service.

When Sunderland Empire Theatre announced that it was set to close in April, many people feared that this time its closure could be permanent. Notice was posted in the theatre announcing that it would close after the show starring singer Jimmy Young and Reg "Confidentially" Dixon. However, the notices did not make it clear if a skeleton staff would be kept on as with earlier closures or if the theatre would close completely. The Empire Theatre manager Mr. Jesse Challons told the *Sunderland Echo*, " We cannot make the theatre pay. The people of Sunderland just don't seem to want it and there will be even less demand for shows during the light nights and warm summer evenings." The Sunderland Empire first opened in 1907 when Vesta Tilley - who also laid the foundation stone - topped the bill.

The Sunderland shipyard of Joseph L. Thompson & Sons was commended by the Journal of Commerce for its achievement in fitting out the Nordic Heron in less than one hundred working days. The rate of construction was claimed to be a British record for a ship of her size and type. The 35,000 ton Danish tanker left the River Wear in April 1959 on her maiden voyage to Kuwait as the biggest ship ever to be built in Sunderland. The Journal Of Commerce commented, "In this achievement, the workers of Sunderland will find hope for the future. Such endeavours are a sure way of ensuring a share of any future building orders for the owners concerned."

Towards the end of the year, the *Sunderland Echo* began publishing top ten charts to reflect record sales in the town. One of the first charts published read as follows:-

1. Mack The Knife   Bobby Darin   (London)
2. China Tea   Russ Conway   (Columbia)
3. One More Sunrise   Dickie Valentine   (Pye Nixa)
4. Only Sixteen   Craig Douglas   (Top Rank)
5. Living Doll   Cliff Richard   (Columbia)
6. Travellin' Light   Cliff Richard   (Columbia)
7. Three Bells   The Browns   (RCA)
8. High Hopes   Frank Sinatra   (Capitol)
9. Here Comes Summer   Jerry Keller   (London)
10. Treble Chance   Joe Henderson   (Pye Nixa)

One of Sunderland's best known characters, Mrs. Margaret Latimer of Harrison Buildings, died at the age of 83 years. Mrs. Latimer was better known by her maiden name of Maggie O'Hare who had plied her trade as a fishwife in the town since being ten years old. She was a familiar figure to generations of East Enders and could recall the days when forty fishwives bought from the fish quay and, as there was no fixed prices at that time, all the catches were sold by auction to the highest bidders. Every day until shortly before she died, Mrs. Latimer made the journey from her home to the Boar's Head carrying her can for a pint of beer which she drank with her supper. She once claimed, "My can is able to find its own way home from the Boar's Head."

When Mr. Edward Heath, The Minister Of Labour, visited Sunderland on 4th December, shipbuilders and ship repairers took the opportunity to impress upon him the need to give tax concessions to the shipping industry in the forthcoming budget. Mr. Heath's whirlwind tour of Sunderland involved visits to the town's principal industries at South Docks, Pallion Trading Estate and Southwick. He told the *Sunderland Echo* that he was making a fact finding visit to the north east but although he watched several of the town's men at work, he did not speak to any of them.

Left
A view from the north bank of the River Wear near to Wearmouth Bridge in 1959.

Right
Gone but not forgotten. A steam engine at Pallion Station in 1959.

The Rector of Whitburn Parish Church appealed to parishioners to celebrate Christmas not Xmas. "X stands for crackers and cocktails with a carol thrown in for a little sentiment," he said. "Xmas is Christmas commercialised and is Christless. Christians must rescue their festival from the world's X-mindedness. 'X' stands for anything and what Xmas now suggests is not Christmas but shopping and Santa Claus," he continued.

An easterly gale with gusts up to 75 mph blew down dozens of chimney stacks and gable ends in Sunderland during December. In a prolonged spate of wintry weather, Sunderland Fire Brigade were kept busy answering calls from people whose houses had been damaged by the gales. Movements at the Port Of Sunderland were virtually at a standstill. Meanwhile, the stormy seas flung their own bounty to Roker beach in the form of sea coal and driftwood. For several days during the storms, dozens of men could be seen on the beach gathering up their harvests. One of the port's foyboatmen told the *Sunderland Echo*, "It is taking up all of our time looking after our own boats to see that they don't break their mooring. The port is all but closed to traffic. The tanker Benno was turned away because of the gales, the Catford has gone up to the Tyne and three ships which we were expecting this morning - the Hackney, the Camberwell and the Accum - are still weathering the storm out at sea." The lower promenade at Roker was reported to be carpeted with sand and driftwood while houses on the seafront had been constantly peppered with flying grit. As the coal gatherers got to work, a spokesman for Sunderland Fire Brigade gave a warning concerning the use of sea coal. "Sea coal has a high stone content and a fire left unguarded is in danger of bits of stone exploding and flying out on to furnishings in the home. The coal burns very well but there is a danger that the users could end up with a bigger fire than they intended", said the statement.

It was announced that the Local Government Boundaries Commission would visit Sunderland to consider the corporation's borough boundary extension plans. The proposals involved the absorption of Sunderland Rural and Boldon Urban Districts and part of Burdon Parish in Easington Rural District. Alderman Joseph Hoy, chairman of the town's General Purpose Committee had been closely associated with the boundary extension plans and he commented, "These extensions plans will give Sunderland the elbow room which it desperately needs." The plans were broadly similar in content to those which Sunderland Corporation had unsuccessfully put before a Boundary Commission in 1950 and which involved increasing the acreage of Sunderland to 23,415 and the population to 231,000.

A three day campaign against rats and their infestation of Sunderland central station resulted in the poisoning of about 270. Although only 59 bodies of rats had been picked up, corporation rodent officials judged from the amount of poison eaten that a further 220 had been destroyed. The cleansing operation was carried out annually by Sunderland Corporation Public Health Department at the request of British Railways. An official of the department said that the work would not be necessary if there was a little more consideration exercised by the travelling public. He said, "Rats must eat to live and if people using the station and trains would remember not to throw edible substances on to the rails, it would go a long way towards keeping down the number of rats." Until early 1959, a station cat - described by staff as 'the terror of platform one' - helped keep down the number of rats but the animal was killed by a train.

Right
A view of Crowtree Road from 1959 whch shows how much this area of Sunderland has changed over the years.

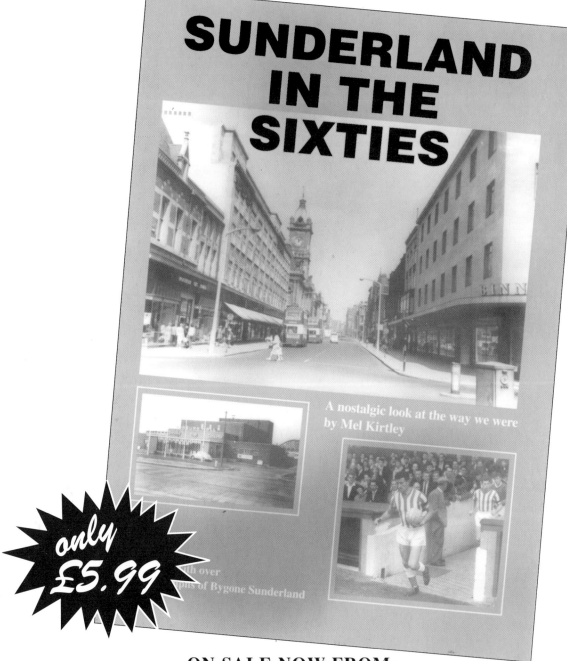